HEALING EVANGELISM

The Medical Model

Published by
Our Written Lives of Hope, LLC
Printed in the U.S.A.

Our Written Lives
book publishing services
www.owlofhope.com

Our Written Lives provides publishing services to provides publishing services for independent authors. For information, visit www.owlofhope.com.

All rights reserved. No part of this publication may be reproduced, stored in a retrieval system, or transmitted in any form or by any means, without the permission of the copyright holders.

Copyright © 2015 J. Mark Jordan

Library of Congress Cataloging-in-Publication Data
Jordan, J. Mark 1948
Healing Evangelism

Library of Congress Control Number: 2015914700
ISBN: 978-1-942923-09-1

1. Spiritual—Christianity.

HEALING EVANGELISM

The Medical Model

J. Mark Jordan

with

Jerry Smucker, M. D.
Carl Johnson, PhD., M. D.
Donald Thornton, M. A.

Contents

Acknowledgements 7

Foreword 9

Part One: The Diagnosis 11
   Overview 11
   Ineffective Evangelism 14
   The Healing Model: The Scriptural Evidence 21

Part Two: The World of Pain 29
   The Basis for Spiritual Truths 31
   The Causes of Physical Pain 39
   How People Deal With Spiritual Pain 43

Part Three: The Healing Model 57
   The Good Samaritan: Christ's Pattern for Intervention 57
   Medical Philosophy 60
   A Philosophy for Spiritual Healing 62
   Soul winning: Spiritual Crisis Intervention 65
   Emergency Health Care 73
   Administering Spiritual First Aid 84
   Symptoms 105

Part Four: The Healing Process 109
How the Body Heals 109
Spiritual Healing 114
The Eight Steps to Spiritual Healing 118
The Therapeutic Value of Salvation 144

Summary and Suggestions 159

Illustrations 163

Acknowledgments

Since its first printing, *Healing Evangelism* has enjoyed much positive feedback from many readers including Bible colleges, district Home Missions departments and church outreach leaders and teams, as well as interested individuals. I am forever grateful for the original input from the First Apostolic Church in Toledo, Ohio where I spent forty years as assistant and Senior Pastor.

The book has been out of print for several years and I have had numerous requests for a reprinting. A reprinting called for a revision. In order to enhance the credibility of the book, I solicited help from medical professionals. Many thanks are due to Dr. Jerry Smucker, M. D., Dr. Carl Johnson, PhD. M. D., and Donald Thornton, M. A. who were willing and eager to provide this help. Their invaluable advice, insight and general tweaking of the manuscript has greatly increased the value of the information contained in the book. Other changes are the smaller format, and the use of the New King James Version of the *Bible* to make it more readable to today's soul winner.

The need for compassionate soul winning continues to grow. In fact, because of our society's massive departure from Judeo-Christian foundations, the concepts advanced in *Healing Evangelism* are even more relevant today than when the book was first printed. I hope that each reader will become a more effective witness for Christ through using the concepts explained in the newly revised *Healing Evangelism*.

Foreword

Many approaches and styles exist in the vital ministry of winning souls for the Kingdom of God. Whatever works for the individual soul winner is a matter of choice and personal preference, but it is also determined by vision casting and achieving prescribed goals. *Healing Evangelism* attempts to analyze the process itself as it plays out in each individual conversion.

The human psyche is complex. Each unsaved person presents challenges to the witness to explore all the possible pathways to winning a soul. Jesus, the greatest soul winner, used many different approaches to those whom he reached. The need is too great and the stakes are too high for us to allow frustration or feelings of inadequacy to prevent us from reaching souls. Let us try, by the grace of God, to overcome any barrier that stands in our way.

May we be like the great Apostle Paul who said *"For though I am free from all men, I have made myself a servant to all, that I might win the more; and to the Jews I became as a Jew, that I might win Jews; to those who are under the law, as under the law, that I might win those who are under the law; to those who are without law, as without law (not being without law toward God, but under law toward Christ), that I might win those who are without law; to the weak I became as weak, that I might win the weak. I have become all things to all men,* ***that I might by all means save some.****"*

1 CORINTHIANS 9:19-22 (NKJV)

Part One:
The Diagnosis

Overview

Sin afflicts the entire human family. This inherent sin incites every sinful act, whether it be murder, stealing, lying or some other transgression. The symptoms of sin extend across the whole spectrum of evil, and cause pain to the soul. In this book, we will view the entire issue of sin from the perspective of disease. Defining sin as a disease means that we can also define the Lord Jesus Christ as the Savior-Healer. Evangelism, therefore, is an effort to bring healing, or salvation, to the soul. Thus, we have the basis for our title, "Healing Evangelism."

Most of us understand the concept of healing. We have long praised God for His power to heal our bodies. The Bible records many miracles of physical healing. In addition to these physical miracles, we also recognize God's power to heal broken hearts, wounded spirits, and depressed minds. Salvation, however, has not often been seen as an act of healing. Usually, we characterize it as a conversion, a transformation, deliverance, or a new birth. These definitions refer to the singular event of salvation rather than the holistic healing process which salvation encompasses. Healing, by its very definition, takes into account the purpose, the process, the prior condition, the end result, and

> **Salvation is healing for the soul.**

the motive of the healer or the healing agent. As we explore this concept through the scripture, we will see that abundant evidence exists to establish the healing of the soul as the central mission of God himself.

> "The Spirit of the Lord GOD is upon Me, Because the LORD has anointed Me To preach good tidings to the poor; He has sent Me to heal the brokenhearted, To proclaim liberty to the captives, And the opening of the prison to those who are bound; To proclaim the acceptable year of the LORD, And the day of vengeance of our God; To comfort all who mourn." ISAIAH 61:1-2

Defining Terms: A Theology Primer

1. All men are born sinners in the sight of God. (Romans 3:9; 3:23; Psalm 14; Isaiah 53:6)
2. Man's universal sinful condition stems from the sin of Adam. (Romans 5:12-21)
3. Condemnation, wrath and the curse of death now blanket the whole world. (Romans 3:19; 6:23; Galatians 3:10; Ephesians 2:3)
4. Sin touches every aspect of man's nature: mental, moral, spiritual and physical. (Ephesians 4:18; Jeremiah 17:9-10; Titus 1:15; 2 Corinthians 7:5; Romans 7:18)

We gain further insight to the healing model by closely observing the phenomenon of pain—what people do about it, what the medical profession does about it, and what defeating pain entails. Spiritual lessons, rich in practical pointers, abound. Through this model, we may understand why many people react in certain ways to the Gospel, and even predict what they are likely to do with it. It helps to "de-mystify" the way people interact with the spiritual truths of the Gospel. By gaining this understanding we can inform ourselves about the process of soul winning and we can more effectively meet the challenge.

The medical model holds the view that evangelism cannot be reduced to programs, surveys, ratios, target zones or public relations schedules. While data and statistics like these may be helpful, they fall short in describing the event of personal soul winning. This book, therefore, should serve as a construct for new attitudes and a revitalization for our earthly mission.

Healing Evangelism has broad implications for our total perception of soul winning, the role model for the soul winner, the procedures in soul winning, and the immediate and long-range goals of the soul winner. It reaches into the heart and mind of Christ, recorded nearly two thousand years in the past, and yet utilizes the most modern techniques and methods in practice today. We have undertaken the task of answering these questions:

1. What was Christ's attitude toward winning souls?
2. How can the church be more effective in soul winning?
3. What changes should the church make in order to meet the real problems of real people?

Answers to these questions will suggest a personal agenda for each church, each campaign, and each individual reader.

Ineffective Evangelism

Most churches take numerous roller coaster rides on evangelistic programs. Some programs are ineffective, some are good, and a few get repeated in the total church outreach. Through it all, however, both churches and pastors long for something that will penetrate deeply into basic attitudes about soul winning. They lay aside most specialized programs after their novelty wears off. An old saw reminds us that "Anything will work if you will work it". However true that may be, it seems difficult to picture Jesus as "working" at compassion, love, caring, winning souls and touching hearts. Yet, that is precisely where we often are as a church.

The healing model seeks to answer some of these fundamental problems that plague soul winning. What person among us has not felt failure, frustration, and even despair at attempts to witness? Many would be soul winners simply give up. They vow they have no ability, no motivation, and no power to do the job. The ones that have some success become dissatisfied with ineffective methods, incomplete results, and disappointments in people. All soul winners battle the negative image that the world has of people who witness.

Frustration and Failure

Numerous studies suggest that within two years of conversion, most Christians stop witnessing. Why? Do they grow carnal and indifferent? Do they exhaust their circle of friends and family? Do they lose their zeal? Or do they tire of constant rejections and retreat into their shells? Failure and frustration compound the problem. Evangelistic programs often seek to overcome these obstacles. Most of us have heard church members sharply rebuked for not witnessing in the following ways:

"Failure to witness is a sin."

"If you don't witness, you must be ashamed of Jesus."

"Don't you care that millions are going to hell?"

"If you're not reproducing yourself spiritually, you're not even saved!"

"Quit being shy. Have you lost the Holy Ghost?"

Jesus never motivated people by guilt. He never pressured people to succeed by appealing to their carnal instincts. Competition, material rewards, threats, ridicule, condemnation and caustic remarks have no place in evangelism. Those who resort to such tactics have a flawed concept of the general mission of the church. Healing Evangelism has the potential to bring hope to those who have given up in frustration.

Incomplete Models

Many images of the soul winners role have been projected to the church. We have been told the church is a sales force. Some contend that we are in the business of marketing the church. Another calls us warriors in the battle to save souls. Yet another portrays the soul winner as a fisherman that needs only to use the right lure. Seminars abound that instruct us how to scientifically define target areas, compile statistics, analyze the demographics, profile people and customize our appeal. Some of the models are listed below. Long lasting motivation does not come from these models.

Agent of Change. If we see ourselves as simply a proselytor or one who converts another to a different religion, we enter into a battle of wills. Winning is only a matter of sharper mental prowess, better argumentation, and a stronger will.

Conqueror. This is an appeal to pride, whether it is carnal or spiritual. Again, strength is the bottom line. It forces the soul winner to continually ask himself if he is a spiritual weakling.

Salesperson. Rejection is the nightmare of the salesman. When we see soul winning as selling, and the Gospel as the product, we set ourselves up for rejection. Success rises or falls on the fickleness of the "buyer." Moreover, the sales model requires us to please, woo, trick, manipulate or trap the customer into buying. For unscrupulous minds, pressure to "sell" the Gospel has even led to tampering with the message itself in order to make it more attractive. Even if some elements of evangelism seem to fit this model, it rests on a false premise.

Pronouncer. "I'm right and you're wrong." This sums up the style of the pronouncer. When you tell people to shut up and listen to you, you eliminate ninety nine percent of the souls you want to win. It is neither soul winning nor witnessing.

Inspector. For this person, the sinner's sins are so offensive that he continually reacts and points his finger at the flaws, much like a quality control inspector who is trained to look for scrap. His tools of trade are micrometers and scales. Before he shows any care or mercy, he is alert to every difference, every variant belief, every misstep, and every questionable move. The Bible teaches, however, that "all have sinned." It's not necessary to inspect for flaws. The flaws were deeply ingrained in us through Adam's sin. We should search for ways to care.

Sportfisherman. Yes, Jesus said we would be fishers of men. He said this, however, to career fishermen who could easily understand His reference. They didn't fish for the sport of it; it was their livlihood, their identity. We must see souls as more than wily fish. Soul winners must be more than rod and reel experts who enjoy a good challenge.

Hunter. Is a soul winner someone with a rifle and binoculars out stalking his prey? Should we think of souls as trophies that hang from our walls? Are we out for bragging rights, record racks and pricey pelts? Not much compassion exists in this model.

Counselor. Our total mission as a soul winner is not over when we help to relieve someone's spiritual discomfort. While we must care about a person's pain, we also recognize that the problem will never be solved until he or she deals with the sin question. Band-Aids are only a temporary answer until a complete treatment is possible. True soul winning begins *after* the individual we're winning has received the Holy Spirit.

Politician. Sometimes it seems that modern evangelism has come down to popularity contests between preachers, churches or denominations. Whoever puts on the biggest show, builds the finest facility, offers the widest range of services, or handles public relations in the most professional way gets touted as most likely to grow. These techniques are not inherently wrong, but they often become the main thrust of the church. They do not mean that smaller churches will never win souls.

Charismatic Personality. Madison Avenue idolizes glamour and glitz. Far too many of us assume that plain looks and average personalities cannot win souls. Smiles and handshakes and remembering names may be prescribed by the world in the quest for success, but winning souls moves quickly beyond such superficial tactics.

The foregoing list does not exhaust evangelism models, but it represents a genre of ideas that appeal to the wrong instincts and emotions within us. Pride, competition, fleshly glory, philanthropy or worldly acclaim cannot provide an enduring reason for the church to reach out to the world. The less noble the cause, the more badgering and pressure must be applied to keep it going.

In assessing the results of an evangelism program, we must look at the impact on both the soul winner and the soul. First, many who pattern after incomplete models may become deeply discouraged by failure and rejection. After long periods of rejection, they back away from initiating a witness. Occasionally, a stirring message about winning the lost provokes them to repent about their failure to witness. They try again, fail, and repeat the process over and over. Eventually, they just repent about not witnessing, but never do anything else about it. Others become radical about witnessing and pride themselves in "telling" people about Jesus. For all their talk, however, they win few, if any, souls. Still others perceive witnessing as setting people straight, winning arguments, scoring points, and parading their knowledge about the Bible. Those who fail at soul winning often say things like:

"I've tried and I just can't do it."

"I'm not the type to win souls."

"I need more training." (And more, and more...)

"I don't know enough about the Bible."

"People just don't want the Lord anymore."

"I'm not comfortable with sinners."

"I always manage to stick my foot in my mouth."

Such expressions are based on mistaken models of soul winning. Efforts that contradict scriptural principles and patterns will produce more failures than successes. In the end, people who once desired to win souls believe that it is either not possible or extremely difficult. They talk of a "burnt-over" field. They believe that revival has moved elsewhere, that no one wants what they've got, that there must be sin in the camp, or that God is displeased with the spiritual program of the church.

Second, people who are won by wrong methods and for wrong reasons often suffer from incomplete conversions and short-lived changes. They make a profession, get "religion," pray, have a religious experience, attend church, buy a Bible, sign cards and do similar things associated with conversion. Deep-rooted sin, however, remains largely untouched in their lives. Souls "won" by a prideful or competitive motives often become statistics on a chart rather than true instances of salvation.

Genuine conversion, however, purges the soul from all sin. We cannot conscientiously preach a gospel that sees anything less than this as its goal. One wise, old preacher put it this way. "We may not be perfect, but our standard is not imperfection!" Salvation may be instantaneous, but it must not be superficial.

Easy-believism, a word coined in the mid-twentieth century, defines a trendy cheapening of the grace of God. Those who practice it desire crowds and outward results at any cost. Easy-believism springs from false models and methods of evangelism. Some resort to this tactic because pressure to "succeed" leads them to sanction whatever results occur and pass it off as a genuine conversion. Some are motivated by their ambition to be seen as a soul winner. In truth, one's reputation is unimportant. The important thing is that souls do have to be saved. Most of us today are tired of ineffective evangelism.

Negative Image of Witnessing and Evangelism

Finally, all of us who yearn for more effective evangelism face an uphill battle against the negative image of witnessing. People are turned off by pushy, dogmatic zealots who are often long on words and short on action. Everyone has heard jokes about certain religious organizations and cults. People make jokes about them because few care to sit through a mechanized performance flow-charted right down to the last raised eyebrow or slammed door. It insults and de-humanizes.

Have you noticed that conversations that turn to religion and politics often end in futile arguments? Sometimes people notify others that they refuse to discuss either one. Why? Because they recognize that not much good is ever done by it, even if they can hold their own in a debate. Witnessing sessions that degenerate into haggling over scriptures, or that go off on the tangent of hypothetical questions actually become counter-productive. Those who insist on this kind of witness make it harder on all of us.

People who talk too loudly about their faith get branded as

"Jesus freaks." In many cases, the criticism is well deserved. Any witness given outside the context of caring and sensitivity is almost sure to spark resentment. Unfortunately, the potential for getting stigmatized is so real that many Christians clam up altogether.

Other practices also give witnessing a bad name. Awkward confrontations, cars plastered with bumper stickers, proselytizing on company time, guilt mongering, judgmentalism and condemnation turn off the average person. In Christian circles, those who reduce their witness to statistics or numbers cause all kinds of havoc. Some inflate their numbers or use questionable means to arrive at an impressive number. The actual conversions become secondary to the number each one represents. All of these indicate ineffective evangelism.

The Healing Model: Evidence From Scripture

Let us examine the scriptural mandate for the healing model. Every enduring program must pass this critical test. The healing model for evangelism grows out of many scriptures. Not only does it meet the textual demands of individual passages, it captures the divine attitude and spirit toward soul winning.

1. **The Old Testament uses the words for heal and healing in both a physical and a spiritual context.**

    "So Abraham prayed to God; and God healed Abimelech, his wife, and his female servants. Then they bore children." GENESIS 20:17

    "Return and tell Hezekiah the leader of My people, 'Thus says the LORD, the God of David your father: "I have heard your prayer, I have seen your tears; surely I will heal you. On the third day you shall go up to the house of the LORD." 2 KINGS 20:5

    "If My people who are called by My name will humble themselves, and pray and seek My face, and turn from their wicked ways, then I will hear from heaven, and will forgive their sin and heal their land." 2 CHRONICLES 7:14

    "I said, 'LORD, be merciful to me; Heal my soul, for I have sinned against You.'" PSALM 41:4

2. **While physical healing demonstrated God's power and compassion in both testaments, spiritual healing is His eternal purpose.**

    "If your right eye causes you to sin, pluck it out and cast it from you; for it is more profitable for you that one of your members perish, than for your whole body to be cast into hell." MATTHEW 5:29-30

"But to you who fear My name The Sun of Righteousness shall arise With healing in His wings; And you shall go out And grow fat like stall-fed calves." MALACHI 4:2

"In the middle of its street, and on either side of the river, was the tree of life, which bore twelve fruits, each tree yielding its fruit every month. The leaves of the tree were for the healing of the nations." REVELATION 22:2

3. **Throughout the Bible, sin is characterized as disease, sickness and injury resulting in death.**

"Why should you be stricken again? You will revolt more and more. The whole head is sick, And the whole heart faints. From the sole of the foot even to the head, There is no soundness in it, But wounds and bruises and putrefying sores; They have not been closed or bound up, Or soothed with ointment." ISAIAH 1:5-6

"'Come now, and let us reason together,' Says the LORD, 'Though your sins are like scarlet, They shall be as white as snow; Though they are red like crimson, They shall be as wool.'" ISAIAH 1:18

"There is no soundness in my flesh because of your anger, nor any health in my bones because of my sin." PSALM 38:3

"Therefore, just as through one man sin entered the world, and death through sin, and thus death spread to all men, because all sinned." ROMANS 5:12

"For the wages of sin is death, but the gift of God is eternal life in Christ Jesus our Lord." ROMANS 6:23

4. **Sin, as a spiritual disease, causes pain, guilt, loneliness and many other kinds of symptoms affecting the soul, spirit and flesh.**

   a. Adam and Eve were immediately struck with guilt and a sense of shame when they disobeyed God's command.

> "Then the eyes of both of them were opened, and they knew that they were naked; and they sewed fig leaves together and made themselves coverings. And they heard the sound of the LORD God walking in the garden in the cool of the day, and Adam and his wife hid themselves from the presence of the LORD God among the trees of the garden." GENESIS 3:7-8

b. Pain and distress was the consequence of their sin.

> "To the woman He said: 'I will greatly multiply your sorrow and your conception; In pain you shall bring forth children; Your desire shall be for your husband, And he shall rule over you.' Then to Adam He said, 'Because you have heeded the voice of your wife, and have eaten from the tree of which I commanded you, saying, 'You shall not eat of it': Cursed is the ground for your sake; In toil you shall eat of it All the days of your life. Both thorns and thistles it shall bring forth for you, And you shall eat the herb of the field. In the sweat of your face you shall eat bread Till you return to the ground, For out of it you were taken; For dust you are, And to dust you shall return.'" GENESIS 3:16-19

c. Loneliness, shown by mankind's separation from God, also resulted from sin.

> "Therefore the LORD God sent him out of the garden of Eden to till the ground from which he was taken. So He drove out the man; and He placed cherubim at the east of the garden of Eden, and a flaming sword which turned every way, to guard the way to the tree of life." GENESIS 3:23-24

To summarize the evidence for the healing model thus far, we can identify sin as the source of pain, loneliness, distress, guilt and shame. These are all relationship sicknesses and are universal symptoms in those ready to come to God. Moreover, these soul-symptoms all lead to a progressively worse self-esteem. Let us now observe from Scripture how Christ confronts these symptoms.

5. **Christ reinforces the healing model of evangelism through His parables, teachings and acts of compassion.**
   a. The parable of the Good Samaritan illustrates that a man's neighbor is the one who cares about him most.

   > *"But a certain Samaritan, as he journeyed, came where he was. And when he saw him, he had compassion. So he went to him and bandaged his wounds, pouring on oil and wine; and he set him on his own animal, brought him to an inn, and took care of him."* LUKE 10:33-34

   b. In His lesson on forgiveness and healing in Matthew, Jesus made little difference between sin and sickness in terms of the divine response.

   > *"Then behold, they brought to Him a paralytic lying on a bed. When Jesus saw their faith, He said to the paralytic, 'Son, be of good cheer; your sins are forgiven you.' And at once some of the scribes said within themselves, 'This Man blasphemes!' But Jesus, knowing their thoughts, said, 'Why do you think evil in your hearts? For which is easier, to say, 'Your sins are forgiven you,' or to say, 'Arise and walk'? But that you may know that the Son of Man has power on earth to forgive sins"—then He said to the paralytic, 'Arise, take up your bed, and go to your house.'"* MATTHEW 9:2-6

   Note that Jesus did not mention healing first. Man's concern was with physical malaise; Jesus' concern was with the soul.

   c. The beatitudes focus on hurting and deprived people.

   > *"Blessed are the poor in spirit, For theirs is the kingdom of heaven. Blessed are those who mourn, For they shall be comforted. Blessed are the meek, For they shall inherit the earth. Blessed are those who hunger and thirst for righteousness, For they shall be filled."* MATTHEW 5:3-6

   d. Christ's self concept was one of a healer of the soul.

"And He was handed the book of the prophet Isaiah. And when He had opened the book, He found the place where it was written: 'The Spirit of the LORD is upon Me, Because He has anointed Me To preach the gospel to the poor; He has sent Me to heal the brokenhearted, To proclaim liberty to the captives And recovery of sight to the blind, To set at liberty those who are oppressed; To proclaim the acceptable year of the LORD.' Then He closed the book, and gave it back to the attendant and sat down. And the eyes of all who were in the synagogue were fixed on Him. And He began to say to them, "Today this Scripture is fulfilled in your hearing." LUKE 4:17-21

"Jesus answered and said to them, 'Those who are well have no need of a physician, but those who are sick. I have not come to call the righteous, but sinners, to repentance.'" LUKE 5:31-32

e. A healing ministry is Christ's mandate for the church.

"For I was hungry and you gave Me food; I was thirsty and you gave Me drink; I was a stranger and you took Me in; I was naked and you clothed Me; I was sick and you visited Me; I was in prison and you came to Me.' Then the righteous will answer Him, saying, 'Lord, when did we see You hungry and feed You, or thirsty and give You drink? When did we see You a stranger and take You in, or naked and clothe You? Or when did we see You sick, or in prison, and come to You?' And the King will answer and say to them, 'Assuredly, I say to you, inasmuch as you did it to one of the least of these My brethren, you did it to Me.'" MATTHEW 25:35-40

6. The essence of the Gospel is redemption.

"Therefore, if anyone is in Christ, he is a new creation; old things have passed away; behold, all things have become new. Now all things are of God, who has reconciled us to Himself through Jesus Christ, and has given us the ministry of reconciliation, that is, that God was in Christ reconciling the world to Himself, not imputing their trespasses to them, and has committed to us the word of reconciliation. Now then, we are ambassadors for Christ, as though God were pleading through us: we implore you on Christ's behalf, be reconciled to God. For He made Him who knew no sin to be sin for us, that we might become the righteousness of God in Him." 2 CORINTHIANS 5:17-21

7. **Physical healing was primarily used to show God's power and to bring attention to the Gospel.**

    "Now as Jesus passed by, He saw a man who was blind from birth. And His disciples asked Him, saying, 'Rabbi, who sinned, this man or his parents, that he was born blind?' Jesus answered, 'Neither this man nor his parents sinned, but that the works of God should be revealed in him.' When He had said these things, He spat on the ground and made clay with the saliva; and He anointed the eyes of the blind man with the clay. And He said to him, 'Go, wash in the pool of Siloam' (which is translated, Sent). So he went and washed, and came back seeing." JOHN 9:1-3; 6-7

8. **Healing more fully represents the entire scope of salvation than does any other definition of soul winning: The prior condition, the act of salvation, the nature of the soul winner, the positive intent, purpose of God, and the generally holistic approach.**

    "He is despised and rejected by men, a man of sorrows and acquainted with grief. And we hid, as it were, our faces from Him; He was despised, and we did not esteem Him. Surely He has borne our griefs and carried our sorrows; Yet we esteemed Him stricken, Smitten by God, and afflicted. But He was wounded for our transgressions, He was bruised for our iniquities; the chastisement for our peace was upon Him, And by His stripes we are healed. All we like sheep have gone astray;

We have turned, every one, to his own way; And the LORD has laid on Him the iniquity of us all." ISAIAH 53:3-6

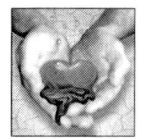

Part Two:

The World of Pain

The Basis for Spiritual Truths

Christ, the Master Teacher, found the world around Him to be His greatest teaching resource. He constantly drew simple parallels between the natural and the spiritual realms in His parables and His conversations with His disciples. This technique allowed Him to relate directly to his hearers because he talked about the things most familiar to them such as sheep herding, farming, housekeeping, and servanthood. He first established a truth in the natural realm, and then applied it to the spiritual kingdom. The Apostle Paul makes this point in the book of Romans.

> *"For since the creation of the world His invisible attributes are clearly seen, being understood by the things that are made, even His eternal power and Godhead, so that they are without excuse."*
> ROMANS 1:20.

The study of natural phenomena yields great insight into spiritual truths for us as well. In order to understand "Healing Evangelism",

> **The Healing Model: Scriptural Evidence**
> 1. Healing is both physical and spiritual.
> 2. Spiritual healing is God's eternal purpose.
> 3. Sin is a disease which results in death.
> 4. Sin causes pain, guilt and loneliness.
> 5. Christ's ministry reinforces the healing model.
> 6. The essence of the gospel is reconciliation and redemption.
> 7. Physical healing proves God's power to save from sin.
> 8. Healing represents the entire scope of salvation.

the reader must assume that the spiritual truths of sin and salvation have close parallels in the human condition of disease, injury and healing. Sin behaves like a disease; salvation behaves like healing. The similarities are so close that nearly each point in the natural has a corresponding spiritual counterpart.

The Causes of Physical Pain

What is Pain?

Pain is an unpleasant sensory and emotional experience that is usually caused by an injury or threat of injury to the tissues of the body. Health care experts know that the behavior of a person in pain must be understood as a complex interaction of physiological, psychological and sociological factors. For example, an individual's response to injury or pain varies from culture to culture, depending upon such factors as age, gender, and social expectations. The threshold of pain often differs widely from person to person, even within the same culture. It also differs based on time, prior pain exposure and experience, stress level and attention to the pain.

In the recent decades, the medical field has stressed patient sensitivity, especially with regard to pain. Health care professionals insist that pain must be viewed from the patient's perspective. Pain is whatever the patient says it is, and it occurs whenever the patient says it does. They recognize that it is ludicrous to tell patients that they do not feel pain when they say they do. The constant report of pain may frustrate the doctors or nurses, but the sensitivity must lie with the patients who are actually suffering. Also, professionals know that the amount of obvious injury may not necessarily be equal to the amount of pain. The severity of the pain is often worse if the cause is unknown.

Pain is often classified as either acute or chronic. Acute pain occurs suddenly, has limited duration, and is usually reversible. It gives a sharp, prickling, "electric" sensation. Chronic pain is deep in origin, may be either intermittent or persistent, and becomes increasingly intense over time. Sufferers often describe chronic pain as a burning, aching or throbbing sensation. Such descriptions aid the

> **Sin behaves like a disease; salvation, like a healing.**

care provider in locating the cause of the pain. Thus, it is vital for the patient to communicate to the health care professional exactly how he/she feels. If this expression is discouraged or denied, the problem may be an improper or incomplete diagnosis.

Why Do We Feel Pain?

Why did God create us with the capacity to feel pain? Pain performs a valuable function in minimizing the harm of accidental injury or minor disease. People who have congenital analgesia—the lack of ability to feel pain—live in danger of unrecognized injury or disease. On the other hand, some people can feel pain so severely that it triggers reflexes which affect breathing, heart function, and blood pressure, with potentially fatal consequences. Prolonged pain which is not treated or which resists treatment may cause intense suffering and discouragement.

Injury and Disease

Most pain is caused by either injury or disease. Injuries are physical disruptions of an organism. A disease is any condition that persistently disturbs the normal functioning of a living organism, whether in whole or in separate organs or systems. Injuries caused by external forces such as a fall, a blow, a cut or burn, are comparatively easy to assess because they usually have outward, visible evidences and symptoms. Many diseases, on the other hand, manifest similar or identical symptoms. Only extensive testing or observation identifies them. Some diseases may be impossible to know anything about, except by their symptoms, given present technology.

The word disease itself simply means "dis-ease," or lack of health and well being. At one time, only gross changes resulting from diseases were recognized as symptoms. In recent times, however, we have understood the microbiological aspects of disease. This finding has enabled medical science to recognize the presence of a disease by taking blood samples, biopsies, x-rays, magnetic imaging,

PAIN:
The *Patient's* Perspective

Pain is whatever the patient says it is; occuring whenever the patient says it does.

ACUTE PAIN
Sudden Onset
Limited Duration
Reversible
Sharp, Prickling
"Electric"

CHRONIC PAIN
Deep Origin
Intermittent
Persistent
Intensity Increases
Aching, Throbbing, "Burning"

ACUTE PAIN

CHRONIC PAIN

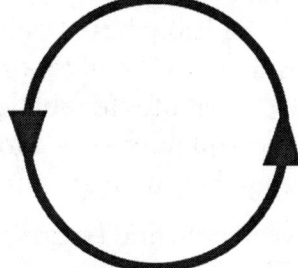

ultrasounds and other advanced methods of detection.

Every organism, without exception, is subject to disease. Cataloged diseases which affect humans, number in the thousands. While we do not know what causes some diseases, we know that many diseases are caused by agents, whether living or non-living, that invade or affect the body. These range from various environmental and psychological conditions, to hereditary factors.

Diseases may be grouped in a number of different ways. Infectious diseases are caused by such external agents as bacteria, viruses or parasites. Non-infectious agents are called environmental diseases. Humans, animals, insects, or substances transmit them. Hereditary diseases are caused by genetic disorders of one or both parents. Degenerative diseases occur as the result of the natural aging and environmental processes. Psychosomatic disorders appear to be the result of emotional stress. All of them can either reduce the quality of life or prematurely end a person's life.

Other Sources of Pain

Injury and disease present obvious reasons for pain. There are other sources of pain, however, that remain mysterious. Phantom pain often occurs to persons who have recently lost a limb due to amputation. They actually feel the pain in the extremity that no longer exists. Evidently, the nerves which once transmitted the pain signals require an adjustment period to the loss. Referred pain results from a physical problem in one area of the body that affects another part. Heart ailments, for example, may cause pain in the left arm and neck. Psychologically-based pain disrupts the lives of millions of people who suffer from mental or emotional problems. Stress, it has been found, contributes to much physical pain. The fast pace of life, pressure to succeed in finance and career, and the stress of urban living all work together to cause much suffering.

The association between pain and stress gives us insight into the spiritual aspect of pain. There are two interesting stories behind this discovery. In 1822, on Mackinaw Island, Michigan, a nineteen-year-old boy named Alexis St. Martin accidentally injured his stomach in a shotgun blast. He survived the injury, but the accident left a hole through which doctors could observe his stomach. In 1895, another boy named Tom, injured his esophagus in a fire. In order to save his life, doctors cut a hole in his stomach wall and poured food into it. Both of these accidents enabled doctors to see the stomach in operation. They discovered that the stomach acted strangely whenever emotional distress occurred. Excitement or nervous tension caused the stomach lining to turn bright red and become very active. The outcome was a landmark event for medical history. It could now be shown that emotional problems impact the body in real ways. Significantly, if sin brings about tension and stress, it causes real changes in the body. Pain is a logical result of sin.

Sin Is a Disease

Striking similarities exist between sin and disease. Here are the most obvious parallels:

1. **Like the pain caused by disease, pain from sin varies from person to person.** Some can sin with impunity. Others transgress only with great pain of conscience. Some are easily persuaded to turn from sin. Others are indifferent, callused or even hostile. Consequently, our approach in reaching people differs from one to another. This is indicated by the writings of Jude.

    "And on some have compassion, making a distinction; but others save with fear, pulling them out of the fire, hating even the garment defiled by the flesh." JUDE 1:22-23

2. **Like pain affects breathing, heart rate and the emotional state of a person, sin impacts body, soul and spirit.** Sin is not merely a legal or philosophical entity that exists only on paper or in the abstract. It has real, concrete consequences.

    "For when we were in the flesh, the sinful passions which

were aroused by the law were at work in our members to bear fruit to death." Romans 7:5

"We know that the law is spiritual; but I am unspiritual, sold as a slave to sin. I do not understand what I do. For what I want to do I do not do, but what I hate I do. And if I do what I do not want to do, I agree that the law is good. As it is, it is no longer I myself who do it, but it is sin living in me. I know that nothing good lives in me, that is, in my sinful nature. For I have the desire to do what is good, but I cannot carry it out. For what I do is not the good I want to do; no, the evil I do not want to do--this I keep on doing. Now if I do what I do not want to do, it is no longer I who do it, but it is sin living in me that does it." Romans 7:14-20 (NIV)

3. **Like disease, sin is not always easy to detect.** Sometimes sin hides in the soul, lies about its presence, appears as something good instead of bad, and eludes the spiritual surgeon's grasp.

    "The heart is deceitful above all things, and desperately wicked; Who can know it? I, the LORD, search the heart, I test the mind, even to give every man according to his ways, according to the fruit of his doings." Jeremiah 17:9-10

4. **Like disease, sin does not have to exist in gross forms to be deadly.** The smallest sin leads to eternal death.

    "But of the tree of the knowledge of good and evil you shall not eat, for in the day that you eat of it you shall surely die." Genesis 2:17

    "Then, when desire has conceived, it gives birth to sin; and sin, when it is full-grown, brings forth death." James 1:15

    "For all have sinned and fall short of the glory of God." Romans 3:23

5. **Like the symptoms of disease, the symptoms of sin often**

attract more attention than the sin which caused them. When the source is removed, the symptoms disappear.

"But those things which proceed out of the mouth come from the heart, and they defile a man. For out of the heart proceed evil thoughts, murders, adulteries, fornications, thefts, false witness, blasphemies. These are the things which defile a man, but to eat with unwashed hands does not defile a man." MATTHEW 15:18-20

6. **Like disease, sin has hereditary roots.** Sin has made man predisposed to further infection and invasion. Recent statistics show that 13% of physical diseases are hereditary.

"Behold, I was brought forth in iniquity, And in sin my mother conceived me." PSALM 51:5

"Therefore, just as through one man sin entered the world, and death through sin, and thus death spread to all men, because all sinned." ROMANS 5:12

"And with many other words he testified and exhorted them, saying, 'Be saved from this perverse generation.'" ACTS 2:40

7. **Like many diseases, sin is communicable.**

"Do not be deceived: "Evil company corrupts good habits." 1 CORINTHIANS 15:33

"Then Joshua, and all Israel with him, took Achan the son of Zerah, the silver, the garment, the wedge of gold, his sons, his daughters, his oxen, his donkeys, his sheep, his tent, and all that he had, and they brought them to the Valley of Achor. And Joshua said, 'Why have you troubled us? The LORD will trouble you this day.' So all Israel stoned him with stones; and they burned them with fire after they had stoned them with stones." JOSHUA 7:24-25

8. **As medical science treats disease without condemning the**

diseased person, Jesus showed us how to love the sinner while hating the sin.

"When Jesus had raised Himself up and saw no one but the woman, He said to her, 'Woman, where are those accusers of yours? Has no one condemned you?' She said, 'No one, Lord.' And Jesus said to her, 'Neither do I condemn you; go and sin no more.'" JOHN 8:9-11

"Now all things are of God, who has reconciled us to Himself through Jesus Christ, and has given us the ministry of reconciliation, that is, that God was in Christ reconciling the world to Himself, not imputing their trespasses to them, and has committed to us the word of reconciliation." 2 CORINTHIANS 5:19

"For when we were still without strength, in due time Christ died for the ungodly. For scarcely for a righteous man will one die; yet perhaps for a good man someone would even dare to die. But God demonstrates His own love toward us, in that while we were still sinners, Christ died for us." ROMANS 5:6-8

9. **Pain caused by sin is registered upon the conscience.** If a person has a damaged conscience, he has little or no sensitivity to sin.

"Now the Spirit expressly says that in latter times some will depart from the faith, giving heed to deceiving spirits and doctrines of demons, speaking lies in hypocrisy, having their own conscience seared with a hot iron." 1 TIMOTHY 4:1-2

How People Deal With Physical Pain

Why People Wait

As pain level increases, life cannot go on without obtaining relief. Yet, the greater the pain, the more stringent the cure must be. For this reason, many people endure their pain until it gets out of control. They dread the very thing that their delay guarantees: a radical cure. If they wait too long, a cure may not be possible at an advanced stage of disease.

At first, many people deny the existence of a problem. They may have secret misgivings about their pain, but openly, they refuse to admit that anything is wrong. This denial is so strong that even when they suffer seizures, fainting spells, numbness, loss of mental and physical abilities and other serious symptoms, they still claim to be fine.

Why do certain people behave this way? Pride causes some to maintain an image of strength. Some fear a show of weakness more than they fear disease. Others refuse to be embarrassed by physical examinations or procedures. Irrational phobias about doctors, hospitals, knives, x-rays, and needles stop others. Some imagine the worst possible scenarios: amputation, blindness, paralysis, or even death. A surprising number allow cosmetic consequences such as scar tissue or loss of hair to stop them. Many who have suffered bad experiences vow that it will never happen to them again. Some believe they cannot financially afford to do anything about their condition. A great many simply say they are too busy and cannot take the time to get themselves checked out. Others do not want to interrupt their obligations to families or employers. Some believe that the pain will go away of its own accord.

Getting Relief

Eventually, people in pain take some kind of action to get relief. This is the crucial point. Will their action treat the symptom rather

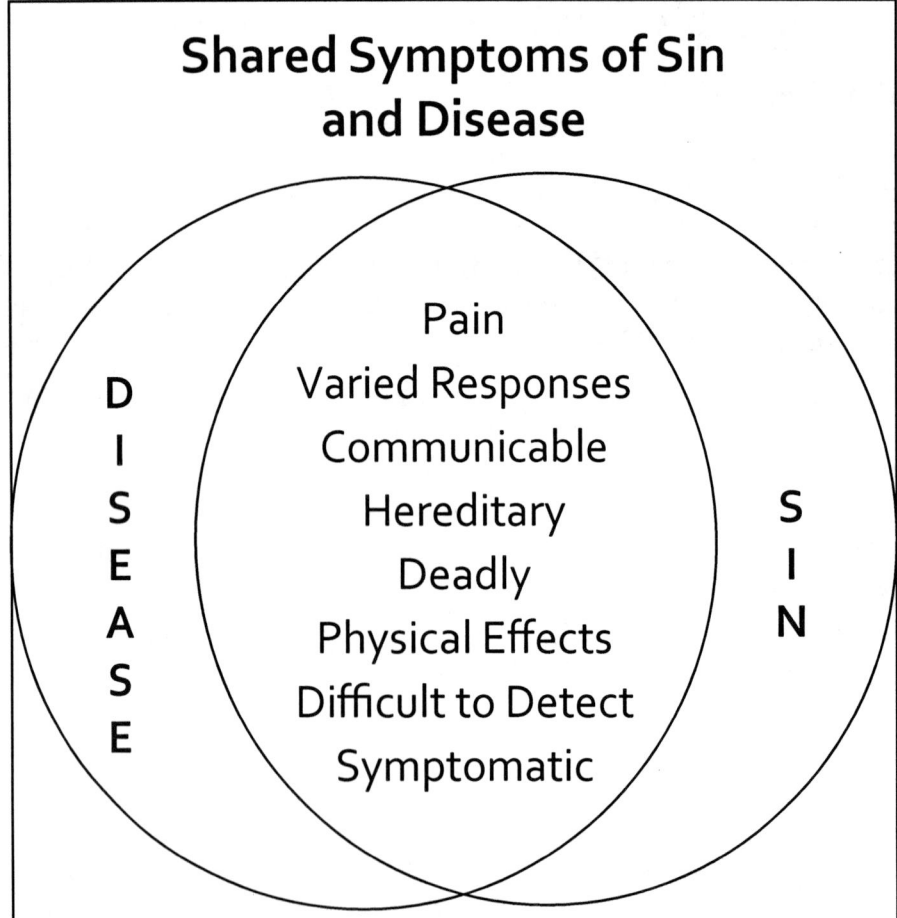

It is important to understand the pathological aspects of sin. Both sin and disease manifest clear symptoms. The sinner suffers the effects of sin as much as the diseased person suffers the effects of disease. Medical science treats the disease without condemning the patient. Jesus showed us that we can judge the sin while we love and care for the sinner.

than the disease? Will it only exacerbate the problem? Will it lead to far more radical remedies at a higher cost? Will they end up as a much greater burden for their families and be lost to their employers after all? Will they lose much more than their hair or their pride?

A century ago, charlatans roamed this country selling exotic potions, snake oil and strange mixtures that supposedly cured almost every physical problem known to man. While the Food and Drug Administration has curtailed most of this activity, a lucrative market still exists for placebos, herbal concoctions, unapproved drugs and treatments. Some manufacturers of these dubious products make wild claims: hair growth, cures for health problems like cancer, AIDS, heart disease, infertility, and more. Why do people believe this advertising? Because pain drives people to find relief. They jump at the first ad they come across that directly addresses their need. Couple this with a strong aversion to proper medical treatment, and a sale is made. Unfortunately, the only product they really buy is the illusion of a pain-free existence.

Common Reasons Why People Don't Deal with Their Pain

- Pride
- Finance
- Embarrassment
- Bad experiences
- The pain will go away
- Fear of more pain
- Irrational phobias
- Cosmetic consequences
- Imagining the worst
- Too busy
- Denial

Going After the Pain

When pain persists or worsens, the search for help intensifies. People eagerly talk about their problem and all the possible solutions for it. If their parents or grandparents suffered from the same disease they may try to imitate their "patented" home remedies. Mystical or superstitious types delve into old wives tales or even wizardry. They collect bits and pieces of advice and try to patch it all together to make it work. Others launch a health food and healthy lifestyle campaign, buying, reading or subscribing to everything they can on the subject. Still others peruse the drug and health aid shelves of pharmacies and experiment with every bottle or package that remotely relates to their problem. Whatever relief these self-applied remedies afford the sufferer, in the end they lose the battle if the real source of the problem is not touched.

Confusion and Despair

Finally, another barricade prevents some people from seeking medical attention—they simply don't believe in it. They think the medical establishment is an elaborate scheme designed to rob millions of their money. With no basic confidence in medicine or medical practice, they will not submit themselves to it. They see doctors as playing guessing games and manipulating patients like pawns on a chessboard, and charging exorbitant prices for it. Unfortunately, these reservations have proven true in enough cases to keep the doubts alive.

Even people who venture into the arena are confused about which direction to go. There are debates about which doctor to choose and which philosophy of treatment to believe. Should people place their confidence in the osteopathic, chiropractic or medical schools of thought? Others are confused about the new emphases on herbal treatments, acupuncture, or hypnosis. Will these ideas work? Are there other innovations waiting in the wings? Will future research discover that present treatments are more detrimental than helpful? People seek a believable answer, no matter how strange or illogical. The proof, to them, is often in a testimony. In the end, many are left to contend with the same old pain that will not go away.

> **Pain drives people to find relief.**

How People Deal With Spiritual Pain

In addition to the parallel between sin and disease, a clear relationship also exists between behavior toward physical pain and spiritual pain. As we look at these reactions, we must expand our definition of spiritual pain to include guilt, loneliness, fear, rejection, and any other discomfort of the human soul and spirit. All of them are symptomatic of the root disease, sin.

Denial

Psychologists have identified denial as a common defense mechanism that people use when facing an extremely uncomfortable or traumatic event. Those in denial may reject the existence of a fact or reality, or sometimes minimize the importance of an obvious fact. Sometimes people will accept reality but they will deny their own responsibility and instead blame others. At the onset of intense spiritual pain, many people refuse to admit that anything is wrong. Even those who admit to a problem insist that sin has nothing to do with it. Such people often self-destruct and their world crumbles around them. Yet, they cling to their denial.

Pride

Pride stands as the worst attribute of the sinful man, and it must be dealt with before spiritual pain can be addressed. As with physical pain and disease, pride stands as a monolithic obstacle to the cure for sin. Expressions such as "I'll make it. I'm OK. I just had a rough day at the office. Don't worry about me," are pride's smokescreens. The fleshly nature violently resists any show of weakness or vulnerability.

"A man's pride shall bring him low." PROVERBS 29:23

Pride prevents people from seeking help. As a result, they lose all they have, pride included. Pride keeps them from responding to an altar invitation, kneeling in prayer, or even bowing their heads. Such resistance stems directly from a prideful heart. In truth, all pride is false. We have nothing of which to be proud because everything we have is from God.

Phobias

Irrational fears seize many people when they consider giving their lives to the Lord.

> *"There is no fear in love; but perfect love casts out fear, because fear involves torment. But he who fears has not been made perfect in love."* 1 JOHN 4:18

Some may fear any kind of relationship with God. In their eyes, He is too awesome, too demanding, or too holy. They may see the worst things that could happen should they release their faith—such as losing their marriages over religion, alienating their family or friends, losing their identity, or becoming a fanatic.

In the same vein, some people become nervous or embarrassed when asked about salvation. Somewhere in their past, they may have been stung by hypocrisy or perhaps were deeply disappointed in someone who claimed to be a Christian. Even worse, they may have been secretly hurt or brutalized by a family member or a false Christian. Buried injustices leave deep and ugly scars. Perhaps they know that a true surrender to Christ will involve higher costs than they are willing to pay at the moment. They may fear that they cannot maintain their walk with God should they start out.

Indecision

When decisions seem too big, many people decline to make any decision at all. They blame their procrastination on busy schedules, prior commitments, the demands of family and job, or simply their own lack of preparedness. People often say, "I'm just not ready," when they want to keep all their options open. A decision means losing their freedom to choose. Many soul winners overlook this motive in dealing with pain.

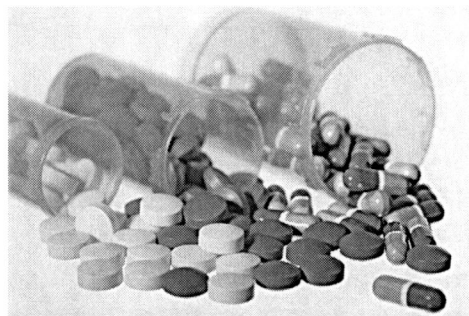

Common Painkillers: Advantages and Hazards

Substance	What it Does	Side Effects
Alcohol	Dulls all sensation	Poisonous, non-specific, addictive
Aspirin, non-addictive painkillers	Disables prostaglandins which "spark" pain messages, reduces fever and inflammation	Damage to stomach, allergic reactions, tendency to overuse, masks beneficial pain
Narcotics	Causes powerful stupor, dulls pain sensation	Comas, convulsions, extremely addictive, may be fatal
The body's own painkillers (mostly endorphins)	Blocks pain perception, causes euphoria	Addictive, alters psyche over time
Heat	Soothes, promotes healing, less effective than cold	Burns
Cold	Soothes, promotes healing, more effective than heat	Frostbite
Massage	Reduces muscle pain and tension	Limited effectiveness
Biofeedback	Pain perception recognition, altered activities	No guarantee of continued effectiveness
Electric stimulation	Blocks electron flow in nerves, can increase blood flow	No guarantee of continued effectiveness
Acupuncture	Blocks pain	Effectiveness may be limited
Hypnotism	Induces sleep, trance-like state	Loss of control, limited effectiveness
Surgery (e.g. spinal surgery)	Immediate temporary relief (spinal surgery 70% better; 20% no change; 5-10% worse or recurrent.)	Pain may return, often more intense than the original pain

Painkillers

When spiritual pain, loneliness, guilt, or fear increases to the point that something has to be done, temporary relief may be only as far as the tavern or liquor store. People don't start drinking because alcohol tastes good, or because it's good for them, or to become an alcoholic. They drink because they want to numb the pain they feel inside, or replace the pain with pleasure. Even those who drink for the fun of it or for social reasons, are using alcohol to address deep needs.

Drug abuse begins much the same way. It often starts out as an innocent and honest try to get relief from boredom, frustration, personal loss or anxiety. Unfortunately, it ends up as a much greater problem than the one it was supposed to solve. The key is to recognize that, in the mind of the user, alcohol and drug abuse are logical, easily accessible solutions to the problem of pain. Drinking and drugs actually makes sense to the people who use them.

People also turn to other substances or activities besides drinking and drugs to alleviate their spiritual pain. Sex, gambling, video games, all forms of entertainment, shopping, descent into bitterness, power grabs, career choices, gossip—the list is endless and diverse. They are prone to do anything that enables them to avoid addressing the true source of their pain.

Search for truth

In order to get relief from spiritual pain, sufferers may experiment, not with drugs or physical substances, but with ideas.

> *"Because, although they knew God, they did not glorify Him as God, nor were thankful, but became futile in their thoughts, and their foolish hearts were darkened. Professing to be wise, they became fools, and changed the glory of the incorruptible God into an image made like corruptible man—and birds and four-footed animals and creeping things."* ROMANS 1:21-23

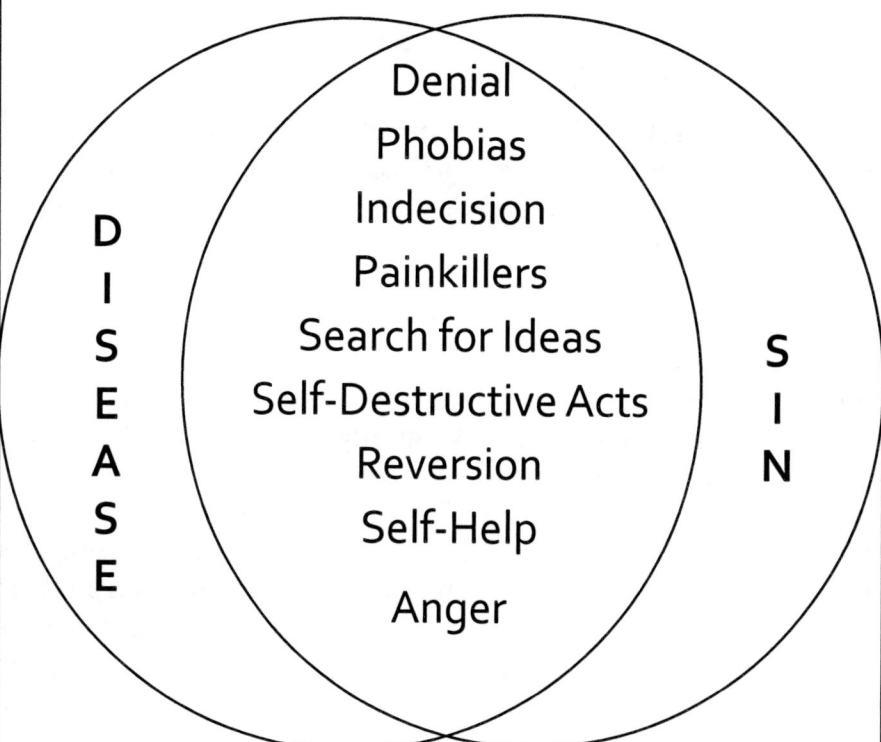

Just as sin and disease share common symptoms, they also elicit similar reactions. This knowledge allows us to discern the sinner's motive for behavior. Instead of interpreting a person's actions as rejection or reprobation, we may see such actions as attempts to deal with inner pain. Thus, we eliminate our defensive and judgmental attitudes and are free to minister to the root problem of sin.

Every year, thousands of people convert to cults, religions, philosophies and heretical beliefs. Many of them join these groups because a deep hurt in their lives predisposes them to conversion. They fall prey to the first group that addresses that pain. A new interpretation of life grants them an immediate escape from their problems, piques their curiosity, and promises them peace, meaning, acceptance, love and belonging.

These conversions seem reasonable when you consider the rallying cry for several of these groups and hear how it appealing it sounds to people in pain. One group stresses eternal marriages and baptism by proxy for family members. How good that must sound to people going through marital strife or who have wronged their families and want to make amends. Another group continually points out the absurdities and inconsistencies in other religions. This appeals to the spirit of bitterness in people by legitimizing it and giving it new targets. New Age groups promise mystical power and control over one's life and destiny. This looks like the perfect answer to those with a poor self-image or a sense of inadequacy. Many groups who have no particular tenets of faith build empires on love and acceptance. Those hurt by hatred and rejection all their lives find this extremely attractive. Most importantly, people usually join groups because someone in the group reached out to them, not because of intellectual or doctrinal reasons.

Few people get saved as a direct response to doctrinal truth. Doctrine becomes a major factor in their minds after salvation, but until then, the most significant gesture for them is for someone to talk about the pain and hurt they feel and use words and images they understand.

Self-help

Just as many people in physical pain turn inward for help and determine their own plan of attack, those in spiritual pain often try to figure themselves out, and then announce their solutions, often outlandish or irrational ones. Psychologist's and psychiatrist's offices are routine stops for these people. They also get ideas from books, movies, television programs, fads, fashions, trends, gossip, boyfriends, girlfriends, next-door neighbors, and other popular sources. You'll hear these people say something like, "Finally, I think I know what my problem is," or "I don't care what anybody thinks, I need to....," or, "Don't try to talk me out of this." They sink into depression while they look for the answer. As soon as they're convinced that they know what the problem is, however, their mood swings upbeat, and they forget their pain.

Pain gives birth to life-changing decisions. Such people may drop out of school or enroll in college or change majors. They may get married, get divorced or get involved in a new relationship. They may quit their job, change positions within their company, change employers or start their own business. They may buy a house, a sports car, a boat, a motorcycle or some type of gadgetry, get into body-building or Karate, redecorate, buy all new furniture, buy a new wardrobe, take expensive vacations, join the Army or move out-of-state. Sometimes they have plastic surgery, change names, go on crash diets, or affect other cosmetic changes.

While some of these changes seem perfectly normal, or at least harmless, the wise soul winner notices them and probes for the underlying reasons. The spiritually healthy person makes changes when opportunity knocks and the decision is pleasing to the Lord. Persons in spiritual pain force changes at inopportune times to please themselves and relieve their pain. The healthy person is happy at any place or circumstance in life, and doesn't depend on change for happiness. One who is in pain always perceives the change as the way to happiness. The more irrational the change seems, the more likely it is a result of acute, spiritual pain.

Anger

Constant, unabated pain often causes people to erupt in outbursts of anger. In severe pain, they scream out curses, viciously attacking whoever or whatever they see as the reason for their hurt. Sometimes they lash out at anything that is the closest target. If physical pain elicits this kind of reaction, spiritual pain is even more notorious for it. Many times people curse God because they see Him as being ultimately responsible for their anguish.

> "But now you yourselves are to put off all these: anger, wrath, malice, blasphemy, filthy language out of your mouth."
> COLOSSIANS 3:8

People in pain often blame others rather than deal directly and rationally with it. Blaming, cursing, attacking, and implicating people around them temporarily blunts their pain. Let's look at several prejudicial attitudes behind this:

  a. "I don't deserve this." These complain about the unfairness and injustice of life. They take special care to vilify God and curse Christianity. They deny God's love, pointing to their pain as proof that God doesn't love them.

  b. "If you hurt me, I'm going to hurt you even worse." Revenge consumes such people. They focus in on a mother, father, spouse, or whomever they perceive as responsible for their condition. Often, they hide their feelings in public, but in private, they dig, taunt or curse the target of their wrath. They know what to say and when to say it to cause the most pain.

> **The spiritually healthy person makes changes when opportunity knocks and the decision is pleasing to the Lord.**
> **Persons in spiritual pain force changes at inopportune times to please themselves and relieve their pain.**

Recycling Pain

As long as the victim aborts the full cure, the pain will only get recycled. This continues until temporary relief becomes more costly than the cure or more painful than the original pain. With substance abuse, obtaining relief requires increasing doses.

c. **"I don't know who hurt me so I'm going to make everybody as miserable as I can."** These embittered souls are virtually baptized in the gall of hatred. They lash out at everybody and everything. Nobody is right. Everybody is hypocritical and out to get them. Their bitterness and anger is the only way they see to balance out the inner pain.

   "Therefore I will not restrain my mouth; I will speak in the anguish of my spirit; I will complain in the bitterness of my soul." JOB 7:11

   "Whose mouth is full of cursing and bitterness." ROMANS 3:14

d. **"I can't stand to see you happy while I am in pain."** Jealousy and envy often find expression in anger, bitterness and resentment. Sufferers desire to be like the wholesome people around them, but are unwilling to confront their own condition in the right way. They end up criticizing bitterly the person they secretly admire.

Gross sin

People in intense physical pain sometimes make matters worse in order to make them better. They smash their fists against brick walls, refuse treatment (including food and water), defy doctor's orders, and act in ways that are clearly self-destructive. Why? It may not be as irrational as one might think.

Damping. When an injury occurs, the body's first reaction is known as damping. Damping occurs when repetitive signals from nerve endings that detect touch and pressure close a "gate" in the spinal cord that blocks the transmission of injury impulses. Gating also occurs when certain pain-inhibiting neurons that descend from the base of the brain are activated. The gate they control in the spinal cord is activated by morphine and similar drugs, and by certain naturally occurring substances called endorphins that are produced within the brain. This process is thought sometimes to act spontaneously during emergencies such as accidents or combat. One may not be acting without purpose then, when he or she seeks a deliberate injury. There is a certain numbing effect created, even though it is temporary.

Sin causes spiritual pain. We might assume that once people realize this, they will stop doing the thing that causes the pain. Unfortunately, the opposite often happens. Very often, they descend into deeper, more repulsive sin. Each time they transgress, they experience numbing or even pleasurable effects.

> *"Choosing rather to suffer affliction with the people of God than to enjoy the passing pleasures of sin."* HEBREWS 11:25

Each sin calls for another sin worse than the one, which preceded it. The gambler risks more and more money each time he gambles in order to make up his losses. The drug user goes from marijuana to amphetamines, cocaine, crack, ice, and whatever else he can get. The flirtatious girl goes from a petting session to secret fornication to openly flaunting sex and sin. The dishonest boy goes from pilfering candy to purse snatching to robbing a store or bank. While each step down gives a rush of pleasure, it is all an expression of pain hidden deeply in the heart.

Sin as a weapon. When people who behave this way believe their actions will hurt those who have hurt them, they often use sin as a weapon against them. They go to great lengths to shock, shame, embarrass and offend those they deem responsible for their pain. They take an impish delight in the outcome of their actions.

Certain gross sins such as abortion and abusive behavior are especially seen in this context. Abortion, for example, is a direct result of pain, according to experts in the field. They say, "Women who seek abortion of their 'unwanted child' find themselves 'socially aborted' long before they seek the medical abortionist. They are aborted, rejected and unwanted by those close to them—their husbands, parents and friends. By the time these same women reach the abortionist they are already isolated and afraid; they feel literally trapped." (Hilgers and Horan; *Abortion and Social Justice*).

Abusive behavior is similarly an outgrowth of a much deeper problem. "The abuser has little self-esteem, often considers himself a failure, relates poorly to people, is jealous, and accuses his mate of being non-supportive or unfaithful. These symptoms are also present in the child abuser... He often vents his frustrations, the hurts and pains of his childhood on his own children." (Graham and Ward; *The Billy Graham Christian Worker's Handbook*).

> *"For this reason God gave them up to vile passions. For even their women exchanged the natural use for what is against nature. Likewise also the men, leaving the natural use of the woman, burned in their lust for one another, men with men committing what is shameful, and receiving in themselves the penalty of their error which was due.*
>
> *"And even as they did not like to retain God in their knowledge, God gave them over to a debased mind, to do those things which are not fitting; being filled with all unrighteousness, sexual immorality, wickedness, covetousness, maliciousness; full of envy, murder, strife, deceit, evil-mindedness; they are whisperers, backbiters, haters of God, violent, proud, boasters, inventors of evil things, disobedient to parents, undiscerning, untrustworthy, unloving, unforgiving, unmerciful; who, knowing the righteous judgment of God, that those who practice such things are deserving of death, not only do the same but also approve of those who practice them."* ROMANS 1:26-32

Reversion to type

In crisis or distress, or in the presence of certain stimuli, the body usually reverts to an intuitive response. It manifests instinctive, "knee jerk" behaviors such as batting the eyelids, sneezing, flinching, salivating, ducking or running. These responses are hard to avoid, even when they are clearly not appropriate.

All soul diseases lead to poor self-esteem. Sin is a crisis of self-esteem. The natural man tries to find the self-esteem cure everywhere (but the right place—Jesus!) The innocent Adam and Eve welcomed God's presence in Eden. The guilty Adam and Eve hid from Him and made themselves clothes of fig leaves. Sin always incites behavior opposite of the will and desire of God. It causes people to fall back on familiar old excuses and cling to ideas contrary to the Word of God. These behaviors are involuntary, unresponsive to reason. They are less matters of the head than of the heart. Often, we hear these common responses:

   a. "Nobody loves me." Insecurity inflicts untold pain on people throughout their lives. They refuse to believe that anyone, least of all, God, loves them or cares about them. Often they lack a definition of love. Insecurity resists healing, and will usually respond only in the context of time.

   b. "I'm not good enough." The Apostle Paul addressed this pain several times in the Scriptures.

> *"For by grace you have been saved through faith, and that not of yourselves; it is the gift of God, not of works, lest anyone should boast."* EPHESIANS 2:8-9

We often think of this in terms of pride, but for many it is an expression of the despairing pain of never being good enough. Such people live their lives desperately seeking the approval of a parent who gave them only criticism. This is not always the case. Sometimes, people have committed sins for which they feel guilt. Unresolved sin brings with it a sense of impending judgment and drives the soul away from God.

> *"But your iniquities have separated you from your God; And your sins have hidden His face from you, So that He will not hear."* ISAIAH 59:2

   c. "I can't believe." Since we are created in the image of God, the human spirit wants to believe. People who say they can't believe are confessing pain. Beneath their callused remark lies bitter disappointment, disillusionment, or someone's failure to build the foundation for trust. Belief is not a feat for the mind alone. Some claim to disbelieve because of intellectual reasons. The more likely truth is that they resist believing in a God whom they associate with someone who has hurt them so deeply.

   d. **"I don't understand God."** No one really understands God, but that does not keep believers from worshipping and serving Him. When people say they cannot understand God, they are exposing pain. Perhaps contradictory standards and rules were forced upon them, or a tragic event in their past remains unresolved, or life has always seemed out of control. Through understanding, they search for order and meaning. Disorder and meaninglessness are painful to the soul.

   e. **"I hate God."** People who claim to hate God are angry for some-thing that they can blame on no one but God, such as loss, tragedy or death. Death itself does not necessarily precipitate this feeling, but premature death does. So does the sense of being cheated or dealt with unfairly. People take it as a personal affront. Yet, they realize that God is the only One who can ultimately help them. This dilemma compounds their pain. Feeling trapped, they respond with hatred towards God.

All of these and other methods of dealing with pain and poor self-esteem are counterfeit. For example, putting ice on a jaw for a toothache, or taking a pain pill will not work. The bad tooth must be removed! Satan gives us counterfeits to deal with pain and poor self-esteem to fool us into a sense of security, but the pain only worsens with time. The sin must be removed, then we must have our self-esteem restored, but only as a redeemed, Spirit-filled child of God.

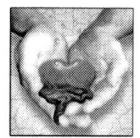

Part Three:
The Healing Model

The Good Samaritan: Christ's Pattern for Intervention

"But a certain Samaritan, as he journeyed, came where he was. And when he saw him, he had compassion. So he went to him and bandaged his wounds, pouring on oil and wine; and he set him on his own animal, brought him to an inn, and took care of him. On the next day, when he departed, he took out two denarii, gave them to the innkeeper, and said to him, 'Take care of him; and whatever more you spend, when I come again, I will repay you.'" LUKE 10:33-35

The parable of the Good Samaritan is an allegorical gold mine. In three short verses it relates the spiritual history of man, the mission of Christ into the world, the purpose and power of God in redemption, and defines the role of the church in the world. In terms of our theme, this parable spells out the steps for both physical and spiritual intervention care with amazing clarity.

The Samaritan's Attitude

"A certain Samaritan... came where he was." First, we must get on the level of the sinner without partaking of his sin. We must relate to him, in his language, being relevant with respect to his specific needs. We cannot redefine the sinner according to our own tastes. We cannot minister to today's environment in the mode or mind set that was appropriate decades ago.

"When he saw him." The Samaritan needed to get an accurate

picture of his condition. Although it was not a pretty sight, he looked directly at the victim and assessed his need. He did not turn away in disgust, nor did he pretend the problem was not as bad as it was.

"He had compassion." The Samaritan did not see an opportunity to make money, fame or acclaim. He did not take advantage of a helpless man. He considered how it must feel to be beaten and robbed. But for a few hours, it may have been himself lying there broken and bloody. For us, evangelism must be seen as an unselfish act of compassion.

The Samaritan's Action

"And went to him." The Samaritan did not offer the beaten man words, philosophies or ideas. He got physically, actively involved in the process. He committed himself, sacrificed his time, expended his energy and executed the task.

"He bandaged his wounds." Open, bleeding wounds demand urgent care. Although the Samaritan may not have been a doctor, he simply used common sense in taking what he had available to him and bound up his wounds. He knew time was of the essence. Before the healing can start, the bleeding has to stop.

"Pouring on oil and wine." In Bible times, both oil and wine were known for their soothing, curative effects. Oil formed a protective barrier and wine was an antiseptic infection fighter. The Samaritan applied the medicines he had to the wounded man. Oil and wine are both types of the Holy Spirit and speak of anointing, cleansing, grace and power. Long before a sinner is regenerated, the virtues of the Spirit of God can bless, indeed, must bless him.

The Samaritan's Aftercare

"Set him on his own animal." The thieves left this man immobile and helpless. He had to have physical assistance to leave the ditch where the robbers had thrown him. Thus, this caregiver willingly used his own resources to transport him. He felt a personal responsibility toward the victim.

"Brought him to an inn." Shelter, protection and basic comfort was necessary to nurse this man back to health. He could not stay out in the cold night. This is a beautiful type of the church's role in the salvation of the sinner. The church must remain visible, functional and strong so the sinner has a place to come for help.

"And took care of him." The Samaritan did not fall short in his efforts to bring a man back from the dead. He could have justified himself in dropping him off at the inn and rushing on to his appointments. Instead, he took care of him throughout the night, paid for his use of the room, and committed himself to the innkeeper to reimburse him for any further expenses incurred by caring for the wounded man. This implies that more treatment and care would be necessary for full recovery. Urgent care must be given first, and then full and proper treatment comes later.

As this parable demonstrates, healing encompasses the entire scope of salvation. Man's sin has filled his life with pain, guilt and loneliness. God, through His infinite grace and compassion, condescended to man's level, entered into his pain, and ministered healing to the soul.

> *"Seeing then that we have a great High Priest who has passed through the heavens, Jesus the Son of God, let us hold fast our confession. For we do not have a High Priest who cannot sympathize with our weaknesses, but was in all points tempted as we are, yet without sin. Let us therefore come boldly to the throne of grace, that we may obtain mercy and find grace to help in time of need."* HEBREWS 4:14-16

Jesus held out this parable as a model for the church. Let us now examine our philosophy of winning souls in the light of this parable. Without the attitude of the Samaritan, we cannot have the kind of results that our Lord intends. As we re-shape our thinking about reaching the lost in terms of Christ's purpose, we will come closer to fulfilling the mission of the church.

The Medical Philosophy

For centuries, the Hippocratic Oath, so named in honor of Hippocrates, a medical man of great influence in ancient Greece, solemnized the conduct of medical doctors upon entering into their profession. Even today, it is used in the commencement exercises of schools of medicine. This oath endures because it conveys the sacredness of life. Every doctor, according to the oath, must dedicate his life's efforts to benefit the sick. The first part of the oath pertains to teaching medical knowledge. The second part, given below, applies directly to the doctor's work.

The Hippocratic Oath

"The regimen I adopt shall be for the benefit of my patients according to my ability and judgment, and not for their hurt or for any wrong. I will give no deadly drug to any, though it be asked of me, nor will I counsel such, and especially I will not aid a woman to procure abortion.

Whatsoever house I enter, there will I go for the benefit of the sick, refraining from all wrongdoing or corruption, and especially from any act of seduction, of male or female, of bond or free."

The Declaration of Geneva

In 1948 in Geneva, Switzerland, the World Medical Association drew up a modern version of the oath. Its text was amended in 1968.

At the time of being admitted a member of the medical profession:

I solemnly pledge myself to consecrate my life to the service of humanity;

I will give my teachers the respect and gratitude which is their due;

I will practice my profession with conscience and dignity;

The health of my patient will be my first consideration;

I will respect the secrets which are confided in me, even after the patient has died;

I will maintain by all the means in my power, the honor and the noble traditions of the medical profession;

My colleagues will be my brothers;

I will not permit considerations of religion, nationality, race, party politics or social standing to intervene between my duty and my patient;

I will maintain the utmost respect for human life from the time of conception; even under threat I will not use my medical knowledge contrary to the laws of humanity.

I make these promises solemnly, freely and upon my honor.

Health care experts find people in their most vulnerable and helpless condition. Very often, their decisions result in the life or death of the patient. Thus, patients expect health professionals to perform at their highest level of skill and commitment every moment. Professionals cannot afford to misdiagnose a patient, prescribe improper medications, fail to anticipate harmful side effects of medications or treatments, or delay proper treatment. In today's litigious society, the danger of a malpractice suit haunts every medical decision or act. But it is a pathetic physician who depends on negative consequences to ply his trade. Beyond the legal and financial considerations, a moral basis exists to motivate people in the health care industry to achieve an ideal. Giving the best possible care to every patient forms the guiding philosophy of the medical field.

A Philosophy for Spiritual Healing

A philosophy is a broad theme, which underlies and gives meaning to a way of life. If the medical profession embraces such a noble philosophy as the Hippocratic Oath and the Declaration of Geneva, soul winners must be no less concerned about saving people for eternity. The Bible sets forth our philosophy for evangelism. As we survey the verses which deal with reaching the lost, at least two ideas emerge. First, we see a profile of the kind of person Jesus targets with the gospel. Second, the purpose of Christ speaks of itself loud and clear.

> "And Jesus came and spoke to them, saying, 'All authority has been given to Me in heaven and on earth. Go therefore and make disciples of all the nations, baptizing them in the name of the Father and of the Son and of the Holy Spirit, teaching them to observe all things that I have commanded you; and lo, I am with you always, even to the end of the age.' Amen." MATTHEW 28:18-20

> "So that servant came and reported these things to his master. Then the master of the house, being angry, said to his servant, 'Go out quickly into the streets and lanes of the city, and bring in here the poor and the maimed and the lame and the blind.' And the servant said, 'Master, it is done as you commanded, and still there is room.' Then the master said to the servant, 'Go out into the highways and hedges, and compel them to come in, that my house may be filled.'" LUKE 14:21-23

> "It was right that we should make merry and be glad, for your brother was dead and is alive again, and was lost and is found." LUKE 15:32

> "For the Son of man has come to seek and to save that which was lost." LUKE 19:10

> "And that repentance and remission of sins should be

preached in his name to all nations, beginning at Jerusalem." LUKE 24:47

"For God so loved the world that He gave His only begotten Son, that whoever believes in Him should not perish but have everlasting life. For God did not send His Son into the world to condemn the world, but that the world through Him might be saved. He who believes in Him is not condemned; but he who does not believe is condemned already, because he has not believed in the name of the only begotten Son of God." JOHN 3:16-18

"Then Peter said to them, Repent, and let every one of you be baptized every one of you in the name of Jesus Christ for the remission of sins, and you shall receive the gift of the Holy Spirit." ACTS 2:38

"Now all things are of God, who has reconciled us to Himself through Jesus Christ, and has given us the ministry of reconciliation, that is, that God was in Christ reconciling the world to Himself, not imputing their trespasses to them, and has committed to us the word of reconciliation. Now then, we are ambassadors for Christ, as though God were pleading through us: we implore you on Christ's behalf, be reconciled to God." 2 CORINTHIANS 5:18-20

What kind of person should we reach with the gospel? Soul winners must not permit prejudice or animosity to interfere with the task at hand. They should consider each person to be loved by God. They must not assign condemnation to anyone, and must always reach out to people with compassion.

What motive becomes a person who leads people to Christ? Soul winners should share the gospel with the understanding that all the necessary authority is given to them. They should go forth with the purpose of seeing lost people saved to the uttermost, and should use the resources of the full gospel to accomplish this purpose.

We conclude that "all have sinned and come short of the glory of God." Therefore, those who have not been delivered from sin are "poor, maimed, halt and blind." In today's vocabulary, we may define them as dysfunctional, addictive, imbalanced, codependent, or suffering from emotional, psychological or social problems. They may be lonely, rejected or guilt-ridden. They may be outwardly successful, but inwardly troubled. The key concept is that people in sin are people in pain. Without a cure, these people will die an eternal death.

Jesus Christ came to rid each believer of his sin, relieve him of the pain caused by sin, recreate him in the image of God and give him everlasting life. He did not come so man could merely exchange one pain for another. He did not come to establish another religion in a world already glutted with religion. He did not come to simply identify sin and preach condemnation. He came to save. "For the Son of Man is come to seek and to save that which is lost." Salvation is, above all else, God's plan to restore man to a right relationship with Himself. We, as the church, are Christ's ambassadors to this world, reconciling it to God. We must incorporate these ideals into our philosophy of soul winning.

> **People in sin are people in pain.**

Soul Winning: Spiritual Crisis Intervention

People usually behave according to their self-perceptions and the way they understand their various roles in life. It is normal for the same person to act differently when he/she fulfills different roles. For example, a man behaves one way as a subordinate to his boss, another way as a fellow worker with others in the office or factory, another way as a husband, another way as a father, another way as a neighbor, and so on. A woman acts differently with her daughter than with her mother. She treats a casual acquaintance differently than she treats a close friend. Each of us acts out our "script" in terms of the way we think it is written or according to societal expectations.

We have already seen that false models, or scripts, exist for soul winners. Such models may have had a measure of success in the past. Given different times and circumstances, they probably worked sometime for somebody or else they would not have survived. In our vastly altered social and spiritual environment, we must rewrite our scripts. The new, freshly conceived scripts must reestablish Bible principles and truths of soul winning. In addition, they must reflect the needs of our times. It is said of David that he served his generation. We must also serve our own generation, not that of a bygone era. This does not mean compromise. It does mean, however, that we should strive to be relevant, effective and achieve our maximum level of excellence.

The Soul Winner Is An Emergency Medical Technician.

In our day, we must perceive of soul winning as spiritual crisis intervention. The role model that best describes the soul winner is the emergency medical technician. These caregivers, sometimes called paramedics, stay on call. When the call comes, they rush to the scene of an accident or to the side of a heart attack or stroke victim with the right equipment and the medical know-how. Their main objective is to stabilize the patient, secure him/her from further injury, perform any emergency treatment that must be done to save a life, and transport the patient to an emergency room as quickly and safely as possible. EMT's are usually not trained as surgeons or specialists. They simply provide immediate care on location in order to save lives. They know that a complete diagnosis, surgery and long-term health care is the province of other workers.

These observations about paramedics tell us important things in terms of their attitude about their job. They do not worry about rejection, about their ability to persuade injured people to cooperate with them, or whether or not the victim will like them. The priorities of the EMTs are clear: to know where the patient is, to get there as quickly as possible, and to keep him/her alive until proper treatment can be administered. If the victim makes the job difficult, the paramedic understands and does not take it personally. This means that they often provide care to the victim at considerable risk to themselves.

The spiritual medical technician tunes in to signals coming from people in pain. He/she remains sensitive to the voice of God in order to know who to help, when to help and how to go about it. Numerous scriptural examples illustrate this role:

> "Now an angel of the Lord spoke to Philip, saying, 'Arise and go toward the south along the road which goes down from Jerusalem to Gaza.' This is desert. So he arose and went. And behold, a man of Ethiopia, a eunuch of great authority under Candace the queen of the Ethiopians, who had charge of all her treasury, and had come to Jerusalem to worship, was returning. And sitting in his chariot, he was reading Isaiah the prophet. Then the Spirit said to Philip, 'Go near and overtake this chariot.'" ACTS 8:26-29

> "Now there was a certain disciple at Damascus named Ananias; and to him the Lord said in a vision, 'Ananias.' And he said, 'Here I am, Lord.' So the Lord said to him, 'Arise and go

to the street called Straight, and inquire at the house of Judas for one called Saul of Tarsus, for behold, he is praying. And in a vision he has seen a man named Ananias coming in and putting his hand on him, so that he might receive his sight.'" ACTS 9:10-12

"Suddenly there was a great earthquake, so that the foundations of the prison were shaken; and immediately all the doors were opened and everyone's chains were loosed. And the keeper of the prison, awaking from sleep and seeing the prison doors open, supposing the prisoners had fled, drew his sword and was about to kill himself. But Paul called with a loud voice, saying, 'Do yourself no harm, for we are all here.' Then he called for a light, ran in, and fell down trembling before Paul and Silas. And he brought them out and said, 'Sirs, what must I do to be saved?' So they said, 'Believe on the Lord Jesus Christ, and you will be saved, you and your household.'" ACTS 16:26-31

People in pain will cry for help. If they are unable to cry, God will speak to one of His ministers about the need. As a caregiver, you should listen for either the cry of the victim, or to the voice of God, and then respond to whatever need you find. A lifeguard does not need to learn a sales pitch to save a drowning man from the water. An EMT needs no public relations courses to apply a tourniquet to a bleeding arm. Caring, compassionate people need not learn clever tactics to show genuine love, concern and friendship. Unfortunately, when the EMT arrives and begins to administer treatment, the victim will sometimes refuse their help. Nevertheless, the caregiver must put forth the effort in good faith.

Training is important, but training must consist of more than how to brush your teeth so your smile will look good, or how to shake someone's hand in order to convey the right feeling of confidence and self-assurance, or how to project your voice to duly impress sophisticated consumers of spiritual products. Training must go beyond how to organize a canvassing campaign, how to fill out visitation or enrollment cards, or how to enter names into a computer.

Training should concentrate on the spiritual aspects of ministration of hope to the hopeless, pouring in the oil and wine of love and grace to those who are bruised and bleeding, and showing people how the gospel will alleviate their pain, guilt and loneliness.

> Salvation is, above all else, God's plan to restore man to a right relationship with Himself.

The Sinner Is The Patient.

The most crucial factor in the healing model of evangelism is to recognize the sinner as a patient, victimized by Adam's fall and Satan's conspiracy. Our traditional view of evil and guilt strongly influences us to assume a judgmental attitude toward the sinner. We tend to assign to him blame and culpability, as though his responsibility for his sinful condition makes him unforgivable. Yet, Jesus manifested supreme love and grace toward the victims of the world. His harshest words were reserved for the hypocrites and religious pretenders.

Again, let us look at the scripture.

> "God was in Christ reconciling the world to Himself, not imputing their trespasses to them, and has committed to us the word of reconciliation." 2 CORINTHIANS 5:19

Examine this phrase closely: "Not imputing their trespasses to them." Looking at this in terms of our model, notice that Jesus did not blame the diseased person for contracting the disease. What does this imply? First, the disease of sin is lethal. Regardless of who gets blamed, if the victim is not cured, he will die. Second, the afflicted person may not be aware he has the disease, or that he will eventually die from it. If this is the case, he is deceived. Once he knows, he will want to get rid of it.

Third, the reconciliation process must begin in the heart of the soul-winner before it shows up in the life of the victim. This runs counter to our religious culture, which has transmitted to us a bias against the sinner. Conventional, cultural wisdom tells us that the sinner must make his move first. He must leave the filthiness of his sins behind and come toward Christ. At that point, we will "bear witness" of his sincerity and reach out to him. But the scriptures tell us quite a different story. *"God was in Christ, reconciling the world to Himself."* Also, *"But God demonstrates His own love toward us, in that while we were still sinners, Christ died for us."* ROMANS 5:8. God took the initiative to start man's healing process within Himself.

The way we view the sinner will determine our attitude and approach. If we blame the sinner, our approach will be condescending. If we feel the sinner is choosing to sin and deliberately destroying his/her life, we will offer condemnation. If we think the person is stupid for continuing in sin, we will harbor disrespect. If we believe the sinner is in control, we will try to wrest that the control away by salesmanship or high-pressured tactics.

The truth is that sin is a moral and spiritual disease. Inherited through the fall of Adam, this disease negatively affects man's judgment, his values, his behavior, and his relationship to God. Pain, guilt and loneliness followed the original infection and continue to plague all of creation to this day. The symptoms of sin serve to compound the devastation, and multiply its evil. Thus, sin causes pain, which causes hatred (for example) which causes strife which causes murder which causes pain, ad infinitum. Spread throughout history, it is not surprising to see such turmoil as exists in our present world.

Our Task Is To Locate The Inner Pain.

Once we commit to helping the victim, we must locate the inner pain. Four vital concepts emerge in this process. First, we must develop *sinner-centeredness*. The soul winner must approach his task with his mind centered on the victim, not on himself. If we confront a person with the mind set, "I've got truth and you don't," or "I know exactly what you need to do," we are almost certain to be rebuffed. Even if we try a milder approach such as, "Why don't you just give this a try?", we are setting ourselves up for a rejection. Can you imagine a paramedic tentatively walking up to an accident victim and saying, "How about a ride in MY ambulance?" These openings result from self-centeredness instead of sinner-centeredness. The soul winner must keep his focus away from himself and his own knowledge until he has assured the sinner that he cares about him first. As leadership expert, John Maxwell, says, "No one will care how much you know until he knows how much you care."

Second, the soul winner must give *priority to the sinner's pain*. From the sinner's perspective, hurt obsesses him. Most likely, he leads a pain-filled life that gets progressively worse. Without hope, without answers, without purpose, panic rises in his stomach. He feels that no one listens to him. No one really cares. Once he hears the well-meaning soul winner doing all the talking, he clicks off the switch in his brain and says to himself, "Here we go again. Everybody wants to talk. Nobody wants to listen."

Prospective soul winners must ask themselves

Focus on the Sinner

Self-Centered Statements:

"You know, you really shouldn't be doing that."
"You don't know your Bible very well, do you?"
"I have the truth and you need to listen to me."
"My church is a lot better than yours."
"You had better quit what you are doing."
"You are just being foolish."

Sinner-Centered Statements:

"Tell me about your problem."
"Are you getting any relief from your pain?"
"I can only imagine what you are going through."
"You look like you could use a friend."
"I like you."
"What can I do do help?"

the question, "Do I really care about this person? Am I trying to get self-esteem by demonstrating my knowledge of the Bible? What motivates me to witness?" Again, imagine a paramedic wasting precious time by explaining to a patient why one style of bandage is better than another, or giving the victim a lecture on ambulance models! Ridiculous, of course. But many hurting, bleeding sinners have died while someone preferred to discuss the views of a post-tribulation rapture position, or explained why the independent churches are much better than those tied to an organization, or even analyzed whether or not Grandpa actually made it to heaven! Strong doctrinal teaching is important, but it must be placed in perspective. Postpone all biblical or doctrinal talk until the patient is stabilized. The pain of the sinner must have the priority.

Third, we must possess a vulnerability to the sinner's pain. We must feel the hurt so strongly, it is as though we were actually entering into the sinner's world of pain. Only here does the spiritual caregiver experience empathy and generates true compassion. Vicariously, we weep with those that weep, mourn with those that mourn, and suffer with those who suffer. "He was touched with the feelings of our infirmities." Christ identified with sinners so completely in His redemptive plan that it cost Him His life. Jesus was the only perfect sacrificial lamb, but we must still be creatures of feeling. Jesus was committed to the victims of sin. Love is not a mere emotion; it is a commitment!

The purest motive for those entering the medical profession is compassion. Likewise, compassion must motivate the soul winner. Those spiritual technicians, conquerors, pronouncers, salesmen and statisticians who have something else as their driving force operate out of an inferior mindset. Christ, in contrast, emptied himself out and acted solely upon ministering grace to the sinner.

Fourth, soul winning must be done in the context of time. Time is a scarce commodity. Most people want to spend their free time with a select few of their own choosing. Busy schedules and the hurried pace of life trample many underfoot. *But meaningful soul winning cannot be done in a hurry!* We win souls through the slow processes of care, love, trust and building credibility. These qualities only mature over time. Wounded people tend to distrust motives and question the sincerity of others. Only time allows the solid building blocks of such traits to come to be. Listening takes time. Bible studies take time. Going to lunch or dinner takes time. Time is the most important gift we can give. This is the most difficult commitment we can make, yet, it is this gift that is most likely to convince people of the soul winner's genuine concern.

> **Requirements for Soul Winners:**
> 1. Sinner-centeredness.
> 2. Priority of the sinner's pain.
> 3. Vulnerability to the sinner's pain.
> 4. Time.

Emergency Health Care

Now that we can see the role of the soul winner as an EMT, the sinner as a patient, and our entire purpose as bringing the sick, diseased and injured to a state of health, let's look at the implementation of our plan. There are two aspects of this model: urgent and non-urgent care. Time, of course, is the significant difference between them in both physical and spiritual dimensions, but urgent cases also cause more stress, demand different personalities, and require different objectives for the patient. We must recognize these differences and learn to adjust our intervention procedures accordingly.

Physical Emergency Health Care

The American Medical Association publishes a book entitled *Handbook of First Aid and Emergency Care*, a step-by-step guide to dealing with medical emergencies. In his introduction to the book, James S. Todd, M.D., Executive Vice-President of AMA, makes a statement that sounds strange coming from a professional:

"Beyond the serious illnesses and injuries, we hope the encouraging message conveyed in this new edition is that many of the first-aid measures we learned as children and now use as adults simply require common sense: washing a wound on a scraped arm or leg, stopping minor bleeding with gentle pressure, or adding a kind word or extending a hand if someone has tripped or fallen. Your first reaction, instinctively, is oftentimes the correct one."

In urgent care, the chances are remote that a trained professional will be the first one to the side of the victim. Lay persons are more likely to be present at the moment of the emergency. Dr. Todd tells all of us that we can do some basic things to save lives, even if we didn't go to medical school, nursing school, or even take Biology 101. The rule seems to be that whoever is present should do whatever they can to help. Concerned people will make sure that what they do in an emergency is right. Todd goes on to say, "And when you perform first aid correctly, it enables paramedics and physicians to provide their care more effectively." In fact, the more knowledgeable we become in providing urgent care, the more we can do the job of the paramedic. (Before going further, a basic medical tenet holds that in an emergency, always take your own pulse first! If your attitude, thoughts and priorities aren't clear, you will be more likely to harm the patient.)

The AMA handbook refers to a three-step set of instructions that should be followed in any emergency. These steps are called the ABC's of urgent care. The letters refer to **a**irway, **b**reathing and **c**irculation. They are the three basic steps in the procedure known as *Cardiopulmonary Resuscitation* (CPR). (The steps are listed and explained in abbreviated form on the following page for illustrative purposes only.)

After taking these basic steps, the caregiver should look for symptoms (a listing of certain conditions, such as pain, nausea, and swelling, that indicate a certain injury or illness may exist). Upon recognizing certain symptoms, the victim needs immediate treatment. After the immediate treatment has been successfully carried out, continued care should begin.

These first aid steps are basic things to check in every emergency. Many other procedures may also be involved, depending upon the specific need. The Heimlich Maneuver (to assist choking victims), dressings, bandages, splints, ice packs, warm towels or blankets and other procedures or applications may be necessary to save a life. Proficiency in these areas comes with learning and experience.

How does the caregiver know what specific action to take? He/she must become aware of the different symptoms and what they mean. The AMA lists symptoms in two groups: common and alarming.

Common Symptoms

There are several symptoms that show up in everyone from time

The ABCs of Urgent Care:
Airway • Breathing • Circulation

Airway: The victim's airway must be clear and open in order to restore breathing. The airway may be cleared by doing the following:
1. Lay the victim on his/her back on the floor or ground.
2. Quickly clear the mouth and airway of foreign material with your fingers.
3. Tilt the head backward to open the airway (if no neck injury).

Breathing: To restore breathing:
1. Tilt victim's head back.
2. Pinch nostrils closed with thumb and index finger.
3. Open your mouth widely and take a deep breath.
4. Place your mouth tightly around the victim's mouth and give two full breaths so that air enters his/her lungs. Give breaths 1 to 1 1/2 seconds per breath.
5. Moderate resistance will be felt when you blow. If there is too much resistance, and the chest does not rise, the airway is not clear.
6. Listen and feel for air exhaled from victim's lungs.
7. Continue with one breath every five seconds. Quantity is important to provide plenty of fresh air.
8. Continue breathing for victim until he/she begins breathing without assistance or until medical assistance arrives.

Circulation: Blood circulation **must** be done in conjunction with artificial breathing.
1. Perform CPR (as outlined above.)
2. Find a pulse in the victim's neck along the carotid artery (by the windpipe). **A pulse means that the heart is beating.**
3. If there is a pulse, but no breathing, continue CPR.
4. If there is no pulse, begin chest compressions. (Pushing on chest according to AMA specifications.)

to time.

1. **Fever** indicates that something is wrong in the body. Most likely, an infection is present. Chills may also precede a fever.

2. **Nausea** is a sick feeling in the stomach and incurs the desire to vomit. Nausea may accompany almost every disorder from excessive eating to heart attacks.

3. **Headache pain** is caused by the tightening of muscles under the scalp, often the result of emotional tension. It may also be symptomatic of infection, high blood pressure or a brain tumor.

Alarming Symptoms

Certain other symptoms indicate serious medical conditions. Trained caregivers need to be called as soon as possible. The first-aid caregiver must remain calm so that his/her reaction does not frighten the victim.

1. **Convulsions** occur as a result of acute infection (due to a sharp rise in body temperature) or a malfunctioning of brain cells. The first aid caregiver's primary objective is to keep the victim from harming himself/herself.

2. **Severe headaches** may indicate the presence of a critical condition such as meningitis, stroke or a tumor.

3. **Sudden loss of consciousness** may mean stroke or heart attack. Perform CPR.

4. **Severe chest pain** may signal a heart attack and should be considered a life-threatening emergency.

5. **Loss of vision in one eye** may be the onset of a stroke.

6. **Loss of sensation or motion in an extremity** may result from a stroke or a brain tumor.

7. **Shortness of breath** may mean congestive heart failure or another medical emergency.

8. **Presence of blood in normal body functions** may signal an infection, an ulcer or a malignancy.

(Note: The medical profession has changed the order of the ABC's of emergency care. We retain the former pattern in this book for our purposes. All the elements are still in place; the actual difference in implementation is slight.)

Spiritual Emergency Health Care

When we pattern spiritual health care after physical procedures, we gain great insight into soul winning. Just as physical urgent care does not include major surgery, long lectures, sudden and radical movements or launching into an aftercare program, neither can we effectively win souls this way. Tragic spiritual deaths often occur while well-meaning people perform sudden spiritual surgery with no preparation or without understanding the impact of their own actions. Some are oblivious to the real needs of the victim. Other would-be soul winners say the same thing to everyone they meet, reasoning that if it worked once, it ought to work every time. Let's look at several aspects of providing urgent care for those with spiritual needs.

Timing. Always perform spiritual emergency care with respect to time and sequence. The new birth message, while it will always remain the ultimate objective in saving a soul, may not be the first thing to do. This is not heresy. It is scripturally sound and can be seen in almost every conversion incident related in the Bible.

For example, let's look at Acts 2:38:

> "Then Peter said to them, 'Repent, and let every one of you be baptized in the name of Jesus Christ for the remission of sins; and you shall receive the gift of the Holy Spirit.'"

The first phrase, "Then Peter said..." is highly significant. It is a time-sensitive phrase indicating that Peter introduced his instructions only after he had prepared his hearers with a vital message about Jesus Christ. We actually pick up the story earlier in the chapter.

> "But Peter, standing up with the eleven, raised his voice and said to them, 'Men of Judea and all who dwell in Jerusalem, let this be known to you, and heed my words. For these are not drunk, as you suppose, since it is only the third hour of the day. But this is what was spoken by the prophet Joel." ACTS 2:14-16

The Apostle Peter proceeded to explain the phenomenon that the travelers to Jerusalem had just witnessed—the outpouring of the Holy Spirit. Then, with skillful use of the Hebrew scriptures, he turned the sermon towards the death, burial, resurrection and ascension of the Lord Jesus Christ. Having been thoroughly prepared, both by Peter's sermon and by the Spirit of God, the hearers asked what they should do. They were ready for the new birth experience. Thus, timing is as critical as the application of the message itself.

This event also illustrates an important difference between kinds of soul winning. God often bursts upon the scene with a spiritual explosion, like He did at Pentecost, in a sovereign move of His Spirit. Through mighty revivals, miracles or moving events, many people are attracted to the Lord. All of us long for this kind of occurrence because it is so exciting, so sudden and so comparatively "easy." Why does it happen? Explosive revivals happen when people actively seek God, or search for relief from their inner pain. God has dealt with them long before the event that finally draws them takes place. Their change may happen instantaneously, but the groundwork for the change has taken place over a long period of time.

But another kind of soul winning occurs in every church too, and it also has precedent in the Bible. We see it represented in the parables of the lost coin, the one lost sheep, and the lost son. It may also be found in the accounts of Philip and the Ethiopian eunuch, Aquila and

Pricilla and their witness to Apollos, Paul and the Philippian jailer and many other Bible incidents. In each case, the soul winner went to the person in need, met him/her in a one-on-one situation, and established a bond of friendship.

Jesus demonstrated this principle with Zaccheus, the demoniac of Gadara, the woman with five husbands, Bartimaeus and Simon, the leper. He identified with each person's pain, initiated his personal ministry to him or her and created an opening for a response from them. Rather than offending them, he deliberately reached out to them in love and understanding.

To succeed in any personal relationship, one person must first understand others. Jesus knew that people who feel understood and appreciated tend to follow leaders who make them feel that way. People absorbed in their own pain cannot receive anything until they feel understood and affirmed. This gives them the basis for faith, and faith paves the way for the real miracle of change and salvation.

Assessing the Need. Before you can help someone, you must find out where he/she is. People and situations differ from each other, and the same process which helps one person may have no effect on another. A spiritual caregiver must determine what the real needs are, specific to the life of the lost person. Here are a few questions which need to be answered before you proceed with spiritual emergency steps.

1. **Is the victim going through an immediate personal crisis?**

A personal crisis usually causes noticeable pain. Psychologists have discovered that the death of a spouse and a divorce lead the list of events which cause stress. Marital separation, a jail term, death of a close family member, injury, marriage, loss of job, etc., also cause great stress. (Two or more smaller simultaneous crises compound the effect.) You must pay attention to this person's crisis. It is a huge mistake to brush this pain aside by saying that it's not as important as

Holmes-Rahe Stress Test

Rank	Life event	Life change units
1.	Death of a spouse	100
2.	Divorce	73
3.	Marital separation	65
4.	Death of a close family member	63
5.	Imprisonment	63
6.	Personal injury or illness	53
7.	Marriage	50
8.	Dismissal from work	47
9.	Marital reconciliation	45
10.	Retirement	45
11.	Change in health of family member	44
12.	Pregnancy	40
13.	Business readjustment	39
14.	Gain a new family member	39
15.	Sexual difficulties	39
16.	Change in financial state	38
17.	Death of a close friend	37
18.	Change to different line of work	36
19.	Change in frequency of arguments	35
20.	Major mortgage	32
21.	Foreclosure of mortgage or loan	30
22.	Change in responsibilities at work	29
23.	Child leaving home	29
24.	Trouble with in-laws	29
25.	Outstanding personal achievement	28
26.	Begin or end school	26
27.	Spouse starts or stops work	26
28.	Change in living conditions	25
29.	Revision of personal habits	24
30.	Trouble with boss	23
31.	Change in residence	20
32.	Change in schools	20
33.	Change in working hours or conditions	20
34.	Change in church activities	19
35.	Change in recreation	19
36.	Change in social activities	18
37.	Minor mortgage or loan	17
38.	Change in sleeping habits	16
39.	Change in eating habits	15
40.	Change in number of family reunions	15
41.	Vacation	13
42.	Christmas	12
43.	Minor violation of law	11

salvation, or to rebuke a person for thinking negative thoughts. Allow people to express their pain.

People in crisis cannot think clearly. Their pain shapes their reactions. Often, they just want God to put things back like they were before the crisis. If they do come forward at an invitation, pray, or seek out pastoral counseling, their objective will probably be to fix their problem, not to surrender their lives to Christ. For them, all of life is defined in terms of the immediate crisis.

2. To what extent are you qualified to deal with this crisis?

We are not talking about professional credentials here. Remember, in the Scriptures, unlearned and ignorant men were the best gospel preachers! (It was because they had been with Jesus.) Rather, it is patience, understanding and time that is needed most. Even though you may have a lot of compassion, you may not be up to some situations. For example, if you have not experienced the death of a loved one, you may not have a deep understanding of a person's grief. You can still help, but you should avoid making hollow claims of understanding. After the basics, a spiritual caregiver's two most important qualifications are commitment (agape love) and anointing (prayer life).

A warning is in order here: some people precipitate their own crises. Their immediate problem may only be the tip of the iceberg. Lying beneath may be a deep-rooted personality disorder which makes them especially difficult to deal with. Caregivers who rush into a situation may be victimized by this kind of person. There are people, for example, who weave intricate patterns of lies and half-truths. In so doing, they generate volumes of sympathy and feverish attempts to help them. Unless this situation is understood, much havoc can result.

3. What is this person's religious background?

Unless you have a specific reason, it does more harm than good to ask a person what church or denomination they belong to. Once a person claims a particular persuasion, they have defined themselves. Think about it. If someone tells you, "I'm a _____," he/she is really offering you an entire set of values and beliefs to analyze. Going further will only waste your time comparing churches and beliefs. If a person volunteers that information, simply say, "Oh, this has nothing to do with being a _____. This is far different."

What you really want to know is the extent of the person's faith in Christ. Does he/she know how to pray? What about basic scripture? Has this person ever experienced true, genuine repentance? Your questions are not for the sake of argument, but so you may know where to begin. You cannot start at the point of one's need unless you know where that point is.

4. Is this a normally stable individual?

Everyone goes through an occasional bout with depression, anger, fear, confusion, etc. Stable people have a good grip on themselves and will return to a normal state. An unstable person, however, has a history of problems which never seem to get resolved. His/her employment record, marriage background, financial history and other criteria are sporadic. People with chronic problems resulting from personality disorders need help, but not by novices or those easily swayed by dramatic displays of emotion, distress or panic.

5. Can you generally relate to this person?

Similar backgrounds often equip a caregiver to reach a person in a way that all the textbook training in the world could never do. If you can understand a person's language (including colloquialisms, accent, and code words), if you can relate to a person's troubled past, or if you can feel a person's deep hurt because you've suffered the same thing before, then you can exert a powerful influence over him/her. Cultural barriers offer stubborn resistance to soul winners. Those who don't have to cross these barriers should recognize their advantage in this area.

6. **What does the Holy Spirit tell you about this person?**

God will speak to you about a person's need if you pray and remain sensitive to the Spirit. He will give you the word of knowledge and the word of wisdom by His Spirit, even as He did to Philip, Ananias, the Apostle Paul and many others in the Bible. It is crucial to seek direction from God in administering spiritual care to people. We can be easily mislead by human wisdom and natural senses if we depend solely upon ourselves and not upon God.

7. **What do other involved persons tell you about this person or situation?**

Find out whatever you can about this person. The Bible teaches us that there is safety in the multitude of counsel. Others who know the person you are trying to help may have some insight or warning for you. Do not dismiss their words in a spirit of arrogance and believe that you will succeed where others have failed. If you feel strongly to go ahead with your mission, go only with great caution and much prayer. God will not help you simply because He wants to prove that you were right and the others were wrong. If you rescue the person, it will be because God honored His own timing and this person's faith.

It is important to check your own biases or prejudices. One provicincial pundit said, "It's amazing how much people know that ain't so!" To proceed based on presumptions or surmisings is dangerous. Sir William Osler, noted for his foundational principles of modern medicine, said, "The patient will tell you what is wrong with him/her ninety percent of the time." Listen to what the patient says (or does not say), listen to others who know the person, and counsel with the Spirit of God.

Administering Spiritual First-Aid

Once you discover a person's specific needs, it is time to act. The steps for physical first-aid find applications for spiritual first-aid as well. Remember, first-aid procedures are not the distressed person's total answer. First-aid removes a person from immediate danger, restores vital life-functions and stabilizes him/her. Continued care should begin once first-aid succeeds.

Airway: Clearing the Blockages

First, the spiritual caregiver must clear the airway from blockages so breathing can begin. In the mind of the sinner, major obstacles stand in the way and keep him/her from getting help. Unless someone removes these blockages, nothing will work. No amount of preaching, teaching, pushing, arguing or manipulation will penetrate the heart of the sinner as long as the spiritual airway is blocked.

The Apostle Peter cleared the blockages in ACTS 8:9-25 as he dealt with Simon, the sorcerer. Peter said *"For I see that you are poisoned by bitterness and bound by iniquity."* ACTS 8:23. The Apostle was checking Simon's ABC's and made a quick diagnosis. It was evident that Simon had no spiritual breath. (He hadn't received the Holy Spirit or he wouldn't have tried to buy it.) Also, Simon hadn't overcome sin (iniquity) in his conversion and he held onto his bitterness. Unrepented sin and especially bitterness are the two major reasons a person cannot received the Holy Spirit. The antidote is prayer, not for the gift of the Holy Spirit, but for repentance to be effective.

Physical needs. People must be fed, given water, clothed and sheltered before we can minister spiritual things to them. This may pose some problems. Transients who are always looking for handouts, or irresponsible people who waste their time and money sometimes discourage us from helping anyone. While we should take care of them as much as possible, there are others who have fallen on hard times and need someone to discreetly provide basic help for them.

Rejection. All of us have seen children who have been beaten regularly by abusive parents. They cringe when any adult raises a hand near them. They expect to be hit. By cringing, flinching or throwing their arms up, they seek to soften the blow and protect themselves. Likewise, people who have been rejected, hurt, and emotionally or psychologically abused, expect more of the same from anyone who gets too close to them. They react by becoming defensive, testy or closed. Instinctively, they avoid any situation which makes them vulnerable.

Countering rejection requires active acceptance. To accept someone does not mean to condone sin. It means to take a person seriously, to show respect for individual choices, rights, and ideas, to let him/her express these views without putdowns, and to show that you are not trying to exert manipulation or control. After accepting a person, you can confront ideas without a big, emotional fight. Until then, however, you will have nothing but a stalemate.

Fear. Fear paralyzes. It destroys a person's hope, dreams, future, and life itself. Volumes have been written to help people conquer this emotion. The people you want to win may be afraid you are lying, deceiving or hurting them. They may fear a negative reaction from a parent, spouse or friend if they should give their lives to Christ. They may be afraid of themselves, the future, or even God.

Blockages to the Spiritual Airway

- Physical needs
- Fear
- Doubt
- Other People
- Rejection
- Sin
- Misunderstanding
- Satanic power

There are two major kinds of fear: rational and irrational. Rational fear naturally results from an actual experience in which a person has been hurt. You can only deal with this by proving your own credibility and trustworthiness. Use the Word of God and be absolutely honest in your dealing with a person. Irrational fear is met on the level of emotion, that is, by showing love and compassion. Fervent prayer successfully combats fear.

Sin. Sometimes people think they have committed a particular sin that is too vile for forgiveness. If such a sin involves abortion, multiple marriages, a complicated sin that cannot be rectified, or even a felony, a person may feel hopelessly saddled with an irreversible sentence of eternal doom. Assure a person in these situations that God has the power and ability to forgive every sin.

> *"But if we walk in the light as He is in the light, we have fellowship with one another, and the blood of Jesus Christ His Son cleanses us from all sin."* 1 John 1:7

Use this and many other scriptures that reiterate this truth. King David's sins of adultery and murder were forgiven. The Apostle Peter's sins of cursing and forsaking Jesus during the crucifixion were forgiven. Also, refer to your own experience and that of others. Eternal salvation is possible, even though individuals may suffer penalties meted out in the courts and in society. Remind the person that the saving hand of God reaches to everyone, even at the lowest levels.

Establish two important facts in dealing with this person. First, does he/she want to be saved? Second, does he/she believe that Jesus Christ can save? If you get an affirmative answer to both these questions, you can then work from a position of strength to help this person.

> *"But without faith it is impossible to please Him, for he who comes to God must believe that He is, and that He is a rewarder of those who diligently seek Him."* HEBREWS 11:6

Doubt. There are two aspects of doubt that block a person's path to God. The first is philosophical, that is, questioning the existence or the substance of God. Don't spend much time trying to prove there is a God. Little is gained by such arguing. If the person holding that view is deeply sincere, then truth will eventually win. You will do better by realizing that atheists or agnostics choose to deny God's existence as a way of dealing with some undisclosed hurt or disillusionment. Their doubt is an obstacle that can be removed.

The second aspect of doubt is practical, that is, failure to believe God's promises. Many more people fall into this category. They believe in God, but cannot envision themselves as a part of God's plan. They need a massive dose of God's word, positive prayer, teaching and preaching. *"So then faith comes by hearing, and hearing by the word of God."* ROMANS 10:17. These people want to believe, but lack the building blocks of faith. Look at their problem more as the absence of faith rather than the presence of doubt.

Misunderstanding. Experienced communicators loathe misunderstandings. They know a misunderstanding is more apt to cause a breakdown in a relationship than an actual event or exchange of words. People misunderstand motives, remarks, gestures, and actions. They misunderstand doctrinal teachings, sermons, articles and tracts. They translate everything they see and hear into their own "language" or personal set of meanings. Misunderstandings are liable to pop up anytime and anyplace.

Unfortunately, misunderstandings seem like gospel truths to the person who has them. Saul of Tarsus "breathed out threatenings and slaughter" against Christians and either had them killed or thrown into prison, all because he misunderstood the identity of the Savior, Jesus Christ. Apollos taught something less than full truth because he misunderstood the coming of the Messiah. Stubborn misunderstandings often refuse to be easily uprooted. The soul winner must do more than know about misunderstandings. He/she must actively look for them and target them for change.

Other people. Intimidation, manipulation or other kinds of influence wielded by someone else may victimize the person you are attempting to win to Christ. It could be a spouse, parent, friend, boss, or a fellow worker. Interpersonal relationships, by nature, are complicated and involved. It is difficult to free someone from this influence without seeming to attack the other person. Take great care to stay out of the middle of a conflict, but put forth a genuine effort to help this person.

First, become a true friend. Your regular concern, shown daily if necessary, will make you an influential force in this person's life. In this way, without attacking anyone, you automatically gain greater power to help shape the decisions that he/she faces. Be careful that you do not turn into a manipulator. A true friend respects another's choices and opinions, even though he/she may not agree with them.

Second, assure this person of his/her own worth in the sight of God. Low self-esteem often causes people to fall under the domination of others. To see oneself as an individual creation of God gives great courage and self-confidence.

Finally, this person must understand that each soul will stand before God on his/her own. Just because we let others make our decisions for us does not relieve us of accountability for those decisions. We must answer for ourselves in that great day.

Satanic power. Satan does exert control over people through possession or oppression. Jesus cast out unclean and foul spirits from possessed persons on many occasions in the gospels. Both Peter and Paul also encountered satanic opposition as they preached the Word. Sometimes Satan allies himself with a weakness that an individual already has; sometimes he takes over a person's mind and body to thwart the plan of God in a family or community.

Often, if Satan is troubling a person, he/she will make some attempt at self-destruction. When the devils entered into the swine in Gadara in MARK 5:1-13, they plunged over the cliff into the sea. The child possessed of an evil spirit threw himself into the fire in an attempt to commit suicide. (LUKE 9:37-42).

Another telltale sign that Satan is controlling a person is a high degree of opposition to the plan of God. If someone becomes vicious, if he/she violently resists the Word, or tries to sabotage God's will in salvation or deliverance, you are dealing with a spiritual power beyond that person. When this happens, you must discern the person's cry for help in the middle of curses or insults.

Above all, do not be frightened of the devil. Jesus Christ defeated him at Calvary. Remember, the only power he has is power to deceive. As long as you expose him and shine the light of truth on his schemes, he cannot work. Learn these basic instructions in dealing with Satan.

1. **Call on the name of Jesus.** Every demon that was cast out in the scripture was given leave by the power of the Name.

2. **Plead the blood of Jesus.** The devil flees at the mention of Christ's sinless blood. Why? Because in order for the devil to possess an individual, he must deceive him/her into thinking that Satan is the owner. But the significance of the blood of Jesus is that it is the purchase price for the soul of man. It authoritatively counters Satan's claim of ownership.

   "You were not redeemed with corruptible things, like silver or gold, from your aimless conduct received by tradition from your fathers, but with the precious blood of Christ, as of a lamb without blemish and without spot." 1 PETER 1:18-19

3. **Pump faith scriptures into the person.** Satan operates in the dark realm of lies, half-truths, doubt, skepticism and unbelief. God operates in the brilliant light of trust, faith and belief. It is essential for a person to possess an abundance of faith in God in order to obtain God's presence. (Again, HEBREWS 11:6 and

ROMANS 10:17).

4. **Pray intently for the spiritual gifts to operate in you.** Do this before you ever attempt to minister. You need to be filled with God's Spirit in order to wage this kind of warfare. Carnality, pride, self-will, human efforts will not get this job done; in fact they will impede your efforts. Spiritual battles require you to fight with spiritual weapons.

"For we do not wrestle against flesh and blood, but against principalities, against powers, against the rulers of the darkness of this age, against spiritual hosts of wickedness in the heavenly places. EPHESIANS 6:12

"For though we walk in the flesh, we do not war according to the flesh. For the weapons of our warfare are not carnal but mighty in God for pulling down strongholds, casting down arguments and every high thing that exalts itself against the knowledge of God, bringing every thought into captivity to the obedience of Christ." 2 CORINTHIANS 10:3-5

Breathing: How To Give Spiritual CPR

Breath is life. The object of physical CPR is to breathe for a person who cannot breathe on his/her own. Breathing equals respiration, which equals prayer! In a spiritual sense, sinners may be so weak that they are unable to make it alone. The soul winner is their only link to life. Here are ways you can breathe for lost souls.

Pray for them. Prayer is the most powerful force that we, as mortals, can employ. Begin immediately to intercede in prayer for the lost soul you desire to win to God. Pray to bind the powers of Satan. Pray that God will give them honesty and courage to repent. Pray to eradicate every barrier to his/her salvation. Pray to gain more insight and wisdom to deal with this person. Pray until you have entered into spiritual warfare, wrestling for this person's soul. Pray on until you have an assurance of victory.

Abraham prayed until Lot was delivered from Sodom. Hannah prayed until God gave her a son. The early church prayed and they witnessed with great boldness. When the Apostles were imprisoned, they prayed until deliverance came. Ezra, Nehemiah and Daniel all prayed intercessory prayers for their people. Paul often prayed for the lost. Christ, himself, offered the greatest example we have of intercessory prayer in John 17. The greater burden you have for souls, the more you will pray for them.

Pray with them. Praying with people is different than praying for them. Just as CPR assists a victim in breathing because he/she cannot breathe alone, praying with a person does the same thing spiritually. As you stand or kneel beside a person, you supply the basic ideas, the words and even the tone of voice as a guide or example for prayer. It may go something like this:

"Lord, we confess our need of you right now. We've tried so many times and ways to find answers for our lives, but nothing has worked. We are sorry for every sin. We ask for your forgiveness for all of them. Jesus, we love you, we praise you, we exalt your wonderful name. . ."

Jesus taught his disciples to pray by quoting the prayer we call "The Lord's Prayer" today. He did this in direct response to their request, "Lord, teach us to pray. He did not assume that they could do it by just explaining to them the theory of prayer. He modeled it for them.

While praying with a person, use the scripture to give more authority to your words. Pray about specific needs that you are aware about in this person's life. It may even help to place your hand on his/her shoulder during the prayer.

After prayer, let the one you are helping know what you were doing. "Tom, I was praying the kind of prayer you need to pray on your own. Ask God for forgiveness just like I was praying about. Worship the Lord by saying uplifting and adoring words to Him. He created us to worship Him. The Bible tells us *"Therefore by Him let us continually offer the sacrifice of praise to God, that is, the fruit of our lips, giving thanks to His name."* HEBREWS 13:15. Praying with a person this way both encourages and instructs him/her. It is spiritual CPR.

Befriend them. Earlier, we mentioned the importance of true friendship in a soul winning context. Friendship is, above all, an attitude. Here are some ways you can show that you are a friend:

1. **Accept him/her as a person.** As explained earlier, this can be done without approving a person's specific actions or attitudes.

2. **Keep everything you hear in strict confidence.** No principle of friendship is more important than this. If a person gets word that you have shared a confidence with a fellow worker, family member, or classmate, you will lose all the work you've invested in him/her.

3. **Express your appreciation or admiration for specific traits, qualities or actions in or by this person.** Many people go for months or years without hearing positive comments about themselves. Avoid flattering, but focus on areas in which you can honestly pay valid compliments.

4. **Be a sounding board for his/her ideas and views.** Take these statements seriously. If you disagree, say so in a non-threatening, non-judgmental way. Say something like, "Tom, let's see what the Bible has to say about that." Or, "Mary, I understand what you're saying, but let's see where that will lead you eventually." The important point is that you hear this person out.

5. **Listen actively to this person.** Communication experts greatly stress this principle. In active listening, you must stop a person after each point is made, repeat it back to him/her in your own words, and ask, "Is this what you're saying? Do I have this right?" This accomplishes two things. First, you are clarifying the subject for both of you. It forces you to clear up any muddled or gray

areas, and establish the important facts. Second, by repeating statements in this manner, you make it easier to remember what was said.

6. **Spend time with them.** Nothing you give is as meaningful as your time. The hurting person is looking for someone who will help bear painful realities. Never act as if you are in a hurry to get away from a person. If you have other pressing obligations, say so. Most of the time, people will understand. Make it clear, however, that you do want to talk with them. Set a time when you can get together.

    Occasionally, allocate larger blocks of time to spend with this person. A thirty-minute lunch break will probably not allow the deeper pain and confusion to find expression. It may take an entire morning, afternoon or evening to really talk things out. Many subjects are so sensitive that they only emerge in the right setting. Time can produce results that prying, cajoling or pressuring cannot yield.

    Given your schedule and situation, it may be impossible for you to give this kind of time to people. As an alternative, consider involving them in your family, job or leisure activities. Can they come to your home for dinner? Can they go with you to get something for your work? Can they play racquetball, go shopping or fishing with you? Once you start thinking about the possibilities, you will come up with many options.

7. **Face problems with them.** You probably have often heard the term "moral support". Anyone in a difficult situation finds it comforting to be with a close friend. Perhaps you can be nearby when a person is going through surgery. Maybe you can show up in court if he/she is in a legal battle. If he/she has to confront someone else in a potentially volatile situation, your presence may be appreciated. These gestures speak loudly. They say that you are willing to bear the brunt of the blows along with your

friend. Words cannot express how much this means.

Many times we shy away from these encounters because we think there's nothing we can say or do. That is wrong thinking. Don't feel that you have to give advice. You don't have to come up with any answers. That is neither expected nor wanted. You can be there, however, to minister on the higher level of prayer, faith and spiritual comfort, not to offer professional counsel. People need to look at you and say, "You were there for me when I needed you."

8. **Legitimize their feelings.** A fine line exists here. We must learn *to affirm* a person's feelings, even when we disagree—sometimes fervently—with those feelings. Remember, feelings are always real, even though they may be based on incorrect facts. Emotions register in a totally different way than does reason. Many times, we react so strongly to the feelings that we blurt out a judgment. This happens especially when a moral issue arises. The person we are dealing with may be looking for the slightest indication of disapproval or shock on your part. Once that look appears, the conversation is closed as far as he/she is concerned.

When you encounter this kind of situation, use affirming words and phrases often. These may include, "I understand," "that makes sense to me," or "I would probably feel the same way if I were in your shoes." It is important for this person to know that you don't think he/she is stupid or incompetent.

You will often find that people already feel badly about certain matters. If you are able to defer judgment and deal only with the actual problem, you may get them to express their own true feelings. While they may be defensive and argumentative at first, deep down they may be agonizing over guilt and shame. The real battleground is probably not the surface issue. More than likely, the true struggle is with the deeper feelings within them.

"Therefore judge nothing before the time, until the Lord comes, who will both bring to light the hidden things of

darkness and reveal the counsels of the hearts. Then each one's praise will come from God." 1 CORINTHIANS 4:5

Circulation: Stop the Bleeding and Revive Hope

Threats to the physical circulatory system involve excessive bleeding and/or loss of pulse. Blood is often called the liquid of life because each blood cell carries food and oxygen to all the body's tissue. If the blood supply gets too low, or if the blood's health deteriorates, this transfer of food stops. In a matter of minutes, death can occur.

Drawing the parallel to the spiritual perspective, sinners may be severely wounded by the effects of sin. When the system that dispenses hope, faith, love, moral strength and other ingredients that are necessary for life stops functioning, it not only signals imminent the onset of death, but healing becomes problematic, or even impossible.

As we know, the absence of a pulse may mean the heart has stopped beating. Even with an ample blood supply, or if there is plenty of food and oxygen, life ends when the heart cannot pump the blood throughout the body. A strong heart, however, can keep a person going long after he/she sustains other life-threatening injuries. Spiritually, people who lose heart no longer want to keep up the fight. All hope and desire drains from life. Without the will to win, or the desire to press on, or the conviction that things are going to get better, there is nothing to do but accept defeat. In these cases, the spiritual paramedic makes every effort to stop the bleeding and get the heart pumping again.

Wounds. What can happen to a person to cause deep wounds to the soul? Without trying to over-analyze, it may be useful to classify wounds into three categories.

1. **Accidental wounds.** "Time and chance happens to all men." (Ecclesiastes 9:11) Life itself can sometimes be difficult. People

lose jobs, suffer broken relationships, go through financial setbacks, and get hit with any number of disappointments in life. These wounds are painful, but the mind understands and quickly adjusts to the logic and circumstances behind them, and makes the necessary emotional alterations.

2. **Intentional wounds.** In contrast to accidental wounds, it is far more difficult to adjust to intentional attacks, such as rape, abuse, rejection, gossip, slander, and other kinds of hurtful behavior. These wounds result from hatred or malice in the heart of another person. The wound is two-fold. First, the actual surface wound itself causes pain. Second, there is the deeper pain of knowing that someone deliberately did it. Instinctively, the victim asks not only what happened, but why. The second question is much harder to deal with than the first. Even worse, loved ones such as parents, spouses and children often inflict these wounds.

3. **Self-inflicted wounds.** Health care experts classify wounds to the physical body according to severity. Burns, for example, are said to be first, second or third degree, depending on the extent of the injury to the flesh. Broken bones get classified into simple or compound fracture categories. Cuts or lacerations may be superficial, needing only light bandages, or they may be deep wounds requiring tourniquets, stitches, or extensive care.

In our application, self-inflicted wounds must be judged as third degree. We must not only treat the actual wound itself, but also we must deal with the complicated reasons why a person wanted to do this to himself/herself. The true motives hide in the fog of past hurts, emotional, psychological and spiritual crises, and ongoing problems. Clear-cut answers seldom emerge from this fog. Sometimes, as spiritual caregivers, we might feel sure that we understand the problem only to be thrown into chaos by a new twist to the story. Suicide attempts, self-destructive and self-defeating behavior should be understood as self-inflicted wounds stemming from complex problems.

How can we best help a victim who has been severely wounded by sin? Physically, a wounded person is in a delicate condition. Sudden movement, stress on the heart, careless treatment of tender or open flesh wounds will worsen the problem. Likewise, the person in spiritual pain may slam the door to his/her heart quickly if a well-meaning caregiver is insensitive. We cannot overemphasize the fact that awareness, care and sensitivity are mandatory.

Love. The simplest definitions of love are best in light of our theme. M. Scott Peck makes a powerful point when he says that real love is "the will to extend one's self for the purpose of nurturing one's own or another's spiritual growth." The Apostle Paul wrote to the Romans, *"I long to see you so that I may impart to you some spiritual gift to make you strong—that is, that you and I may be mutually encouraged by each other's faith."* ROMANS 1:11-12.

This leaves no room for selfishness, manipulation, or any gesture that is not beneficial to the other person's spiritual well being. What do we mean, then, when we say that a soul winner must love the person he/she desires to win to Christ? The following words help articulate this meaning.

1. **Commitment.** Commit yourself, not to the whim, favor or goodwill of the person, but to his/her salvation and spiritual healing. While you must use tact and discretion, you should never compromise the ultimate solution for the person simply because you fear you might be offensive or be rejected.

2. **Giving.** "For God so loved. . . that He gave." Giving grows out of loving. Give of yourself, your time, your moral support, your spiritual strength, even your physical help, if necessary. Guard against being manipulated, however, because there are people who will use anyone they can for their own selfish aims. Tie all your efforts back to spiritual goals for this person.

3. **Unqualified acceptance.** Love like Jesus loved. He declined to condemn a woman taken in the act of adultery. He ate in the house of sinners. He permitted Mary Magdalene, a known prostitute, to wash His feet. He touched a funeral bier—an act forbidden to a rabbi—in order to raise a widow's son from the dead. He entered into a cemetery, another act forbidden to a rabbi, in order to raise Lazarus. He let anyone touch him, He healed on the Sabbath, He mingled with the rabble, and He continually shocked the religious hierarchy by His unorthodox approaches. *Yet, Jesus never condoned sin.* He made a distinction between the sin and the sinner, and determined to show that He loved souls who were debilitated and ruined by sin, even while He disdained their sin.

4. **Compassion.** Love, as a positive emotion, extends from your heart to the person in pain. Compassion, however, enables you to receive that pain into your own heart, as though you were the one suffering. In fact, the literal meaning of compassion is "to suffer with someone." When the hurting person looks into your eyes, can he/she see that you are absorbing the pain? Compassion animates your prayer life. Without it, you cannot carry the burden for the lost and intercede for them.

5. **Go to bat for them.** When an injured person bleeds profusely, someone must apply firm pressure at the point of the wound. In case life or limb is threatened, tourniquets may be required. A victim can only suffer the loss of blood for a limited time. Urgency is of the essence.

In a spiritual emergency, you may need to step into a crisis swirling around a person and take over until you find an immediate solution. This may mean keeping someone on the phone until he/she calms down, taking a person out to lunch, keeping someone overnight, or helping to work out a temporary plan to get a person through a crisis. If you have good communication skills, you may need to mediate between this person and other people. You may need to provide contacts for a person, give him/her transportation, or do whatever is necessary to stop the bleeding.

Because this kind of intervention may be awkward, delicate or even dangerous, you ought to keep some guidelines firmly in mind. Never help a person to do something wrong, even if you are begged to do it. In case you are helping a minor, never oppose the parent or guardian unless a crime is involved. Explain that your purpose is only positive and helpful. In marital disputes, take a person in only if you have reason to believe that his/her life or safety is in real and present danger. Never give legal, medical or financial advice unless you have professional credentials. Even with these constraints, however, you can continue to do many practical things that will mean much to the person you want to win to Christ.

Heart. In order to understand the heart from a spiritual perspective, let's look at the physical organ we call the heart. The human heart is a specialized, four-chambered muscle that maintains blood flow in the circulatory system. Blood supplies food and oxygen to the cells of the body for their life needs and removes the waste products of their chemical processes. Blood also helps to maintain a consistent body temperature, circulate hormones, and fight infections. The brain cells are very dependent on a constant supply of oxygen. If the circulation to the brain is stopped, death is imminent.

The role of the heart has long been understood to be vital for life itself. The scriptures use the heart to mean the seat of the soul. Other ancient writers thought it was the center of love, courage, joy, and sadness. Primitive man must have been aware of the heartbeat and probably recognized the heart as an organ whose malfunction could cause sudden death.

Metaphorically, if someone "loses heart," we mean that he/she has no more motivation or inspiration to go on. Someone may be in a race, a fight to save a marriage, a competitive struggle for a position or a job, or even in a battle against a life-threatening disease. Suddenly, this person simply quits. It is as if somebody turns off the switch and everything grows dark. "I can't go on" and "it's no use," and other negative phrases are heard. This person loses the required strength and willingness to face life. Hope for future goals disappear. Nothing seems like it's worth the effort. When this happens, one virtually ceases to live.

Without the heart to go on, life either becomes meaningless or impossible. Unsaved people frequently battle with overwhelming despair. Some sink into a sea of melancholia. Others grow cynical about all the people and circumstances around them. Still others retreat into self-pity. If these symptoms reach a severe point, such people may suffer clinical depression. The caregiver should respond with alarm if a person experiences extreme sadness, pessimism, guilt, self-dislike, self-accusation or suicidal ideas, which persist for a long period and interrupt the normal functioning of life. If so, professional help may be in order. The soul winner must not play amateur psychologist or psychiatrist.

What should the spiritual caregiver do, then, to help a person who loses heart? Let's concentrate on three areas: the worthwhileness of life, the love of God which involves God's specific will for each life, and life really does get better with Christ as Lord. In each area, you must give hope, show faith and express your belief in God's power.

Life is worthwhile. People who lose heart may despair of life. If talk of suicide comes up, counter it firmly by using scriptures, which show that life is God's gift. Again, unless you are a skilled or professional counselor, avoid getting into the depths of a person's problems. You will do far better by staying in the province of scripture and prayer.

> "Then God said, 'Let Us make man in Our image, according to Our likeness; let them have dominion over the fish of the sea, over the birds of the air, and over the cattle, over all the earth

and over every creeping thing that creeps on the earth.' So God created man in His own image; in the image of God He created him; male and female He created them." GENESIS 1:26-27

"I will praise You, for I am fearfully and wonderfully made; marvelous are Your works, and that my soul knows very well." PSALM 139:14

"You shall not murder." DEUTERONOMY 5:17

"You have granted me life and favor, and Your care has preserved my spirit." JOB 10:12

Often, a person contemplating suicide seeks for "permission" from someone he/she trusts. That's why you should show that the Bible expressly forbids it. This places an enormous barrier in the way. Next, it is important to show that life is not only worth saving, but it is worth living. These scriptures can help demonstrate this.

"Before I formed you in the womb I knew you; Before you were born I sanctified you; I ordained you a prophet to the nations;" "'Do not be afraid of their faces, for I am with you to deliver you,' says the LORD.

Then the LORD put forth His hand and touched my mouth, and the LORD said to me: "Behold, I have put My words in your mouth. See, I have this day set you over the nations and over the kingdoms, to root out and to pull down, to destroy and to throw down, to build and to plant.'" JEREMIAH 1:5, 8-10

The Love of God. Assure the people you deal with that God's unselfish, eternal love includes them. While they may not believe that God hates them, they may feel ignored, left out, or that they are non-persons. Without an assurance of God's love, they have no deep-rooted sense of security or purpose in life. Communicate the following truths:

1. **God is love.**
2. **God uniquely created each person.**

3. God loves man in spite of sin.
4. Love caused God to find a way to redeem man from sin.
5. God provides for each person.
6. Every good gift comes from God.
7. God's love is unsolicited and voluntary.
8. God's love is unconditional.
9. God's love is eternal.

As you share these truths, you offer hope, encouragement and affirmation. Keep in mind that those you talk to may have never had anything but abuse, put-downs and neglect given to them. Your message of love and hope can become a powerful force in their lives. Here are some scriptures that express God's love to man.

> "Greater love has no one than this, than to lay down one's life for his friends." JOHN 15:13

> "But God demonstrates His own love toward us, in that while we were still sinners, Christ died for us." ROMANS 5:8

> "Who shall separate us from the love of Christ? Shall tribulation, or distress, or persecution, or famine, or nakedness, or peril, or sword?" "Yet in all these things we are more than conquerors through Him who loved us. For I am persuaded that neither death nor life, nor angels nor principalities nor powers, nor things present nor things to come, nor height nor depth, nor any other created thing, shall be able to separate us from the love of God which is in Christ Jesus our Lord." ROMANS 8:35, 37-39

> "By this we know love, because He laid down His life for us. And we also ought to lay down our lives for the brethren." 1 JOHN 3:16

"In this is love, not that we loved God, but that He loved us and sent His Son to be the propitiation for our sins." 1 JOHN 4:10

The Word of God and your own words, combined with your attention and kind action massage the heart back into activity. When the blood starts flowing, temperature will rise, color will return and the victim will experience a renewed desire for life.

Life always gets better when Jesus becomes Lord. When people are in the grip of pain and despair, they tend to develop negative attitudes about their lives in general. It appears to them that everything is bad and getting worse. Present frustrations get blown out of proportion and destroy all hope for the future.

The soul winner must counteract these negative feelings with the Word of God. Assure this person that his/her life will be vastly different the moment Jesus Christ becomes Savior and Lord. Point out the positive changes that Jesus makes in a believer's life. Even if this person stubbornly resists such positive talk, do it anyway. Do not back down. A soul winner must commit to being an unmovable fortress of strength for the benefit of the lost.

Plenty of scripture verses lend themselves to this effort. Learn some of them to help you show a person that his/her life will improve after salvation. Here are a few of them.

> *"On the last and greatest day of the Feast, Jesus stood and said in a loud voice, 'If anyone is thirsty, let him come to me and drink. Whoever believes in me, as the Scripture has said, streams of living water will flow from within him.'"* JOHN 7:37-39

> *"I am the gate; whoever enters through me will be saved. He will come in and go out, and find pasture. The thief comes only to steal and kill and destroy; I have come that they may have life, and have it to the full."* JOHN 10:9-10

> *"Come to me, all you who are weary and burdened, and I will give you rest. Take my yoke upon you and learn from me,*

for I am gentle and humble in heart, and you will find rest for your souls. For my yoke is easy and my burden is light." MATTHEW 11:28-30

Symptoms

Symptoms of Sin

Physically, a symptom is a visceral, direct manifestation of a disease or injury and is typically uniform from person to person. A reaction, on the other hand, is a behavior in response to the pain or discomfort caused by the disease. We have already discussed in detail how people react to spiritual pain. Denial, phobias, indecision, use of painkillers, etc., describe these reactions. The difference between reactions and symptoms may be understood in this way. When people develop stomach ulcers, they manifest such symptoms as severe abdominal pain, especially after eating certain foods, and may notice signs of bleeding from the intestinal tract. These are symptoms. These same people, however, may clutch their stomachs and bend over, cry out from the pain, drink milk to sooth the inflammation, or do something else to relieve the pain. These are reactions. Reactions vary from person to person, and many times are simply choices. Symptoms are involuntary and automatic.

The inherent sinful nature manifests itself by various acts or symptoms of sin. Sinners commit individual sins involuntarily because of their sinful condition. People in sin automatically develop guilt, shame, loneliness, pain and emptiness as a by-product of sin. The scriptures give us several catalogs of sin which define these behaviors. All of them result from a sinful heart.

> *"And even as they did not like to retain God in their knowledge, God gave them over to a debased mind, to do those things which are not fitting; being filled with all unrighteousness, sexual immorality, wickedness, covetousness, maliciousness; full of envy, murder, strife, deceit, evil-mindedness; they are whisperers, backbiters, haters of God, violent, proud, boasters, inventors of evil things, disobedient to parents, undiscerning, untrustworthy, unloving, unforgiving, unmerciful; who, knowing the righteous judgment of God, that those who practice such*

things are deserving of death, not only do the same but also approve of those who practice them." ROMANS 1:28-32

In the Galatian epistle, these sins are described as the works of the flesh. Any person who walks in the flesh instead of in the Spirit will manifest telltale signs.

"Now the works of the flesh are evident, which are: adultery, fornication, uncleanness, lewdness, idolatry, sorcery, hatred, contentions, jealousies, outbursts of wrath, selfish ambitions, dissensions, heresies, envy, murders, drunkenness, revelries, and the like; of which I tell you beforehand, just as I also told you in time past, that those who practice such things will not inherit the kingdom of God." GALATIANS 5:19-21

It must be abundantly clear that the underlying culprit in all these areas remains the basic sinful nature of man. We must not succumb to the false, humanistic ideas that the problem is the social milieu, the cultural mix, or the "oppressive" tradition of religious influence. Social programs may help alleviate some injustice, pain and suffering. As long as sin exists, however, the root of evil will continue to produce harm.

Signs of Spiritual Activity

The first-aid caregiver must not only learn to detect symptoms, it is also important to know whether the treatment is working. Spiritually, the soul winner should be able to see the results of spiritual first-aid. The gospel always brings some kind of reaction from people. If it is received in faith, the seed of the Word will germinate and begin to grow. If it is rejected, it will manifest signs of that as well. Here are some scriptural examples of spiritual activity that resulted when people heard the Gospel.

"Now when they heard this, they were cut to the heart, and said to Peter and the rest of the apostles, 'Men and brethren, what shall we do?'" ACTS 2:37

> "While Peter was still speaking these words, the Holy Spirit fell upon all those who heard the word." ACTS 10:44

> "Now as he reasoned about righteousness, self-control, and the judgment to come, Felix was afraid and answered, 'Go away for now; when I have a convenient time I will call for you.'" ACTS 24:25

People sometimes become very agitated when the gospel is preached to them and they resist it. Our term for this is "conviction of the Spirit." In other words, they feel a great deal of guilt and realize that they must make a decision. They are unwilling to act, however, in accordance with the will of God. In family situations, a person who is "under conviction" may show great irritation, erupt in fits of rage, start arguments or make life miserable for everybody in the family. In the workplace, a person who rejects the truth may cast insults, ridicule, or even plot to cause a believer to lose his/her job. Such behavior stems from resisting the work of the Spirit in that person's life. The soul winner must take great care to react to each incident in a positive, loving way. Of course, even a Christian does not have to jeopardize a good job or position if a righteous and fair recourse is open, but whatever happens, integrity and honor must be preserved. The desire for revenge should never poison the heart of a believer.

Finally, be patient. Your witness may not bear fruit immediately. In fact, in many cases, years pass by before someone acts on a gospel message or witness. Do not ruin the painstaking efforts out of exasperation. Patience is not wasting time; it is informed waiting. Your efforts may still pay off some time in the future.

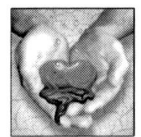

Part Four:

The Healing Process

How the Body Heals

Our Creator fashioned a marvelous physical body for mankind. In its normal, healthy state, it works ingeniously to sustain our life. But that's only the beginning. When disease or injury threatens, its built-in powers multiply, turning the human physique into a mighty army. It calls up lines of defense, maneuvers units into place to launch a counter-attack and destroy invaders, invokes emergency procedures to beef up supply lines and transport troops and munitions, and restores damages and losses. As we look at how the body heals, we will receive a great education on the spiritual aspects of healing.

The Four Lines of Defense

"An ounce of prevention is worth a pound of cure." This old adage accurately describes the strategy that the body employs when fighting against disease. Our bodies come equipped with four major lines of defense: primary protection, the combative response, the inflammatory response and the immune response. These systems work together to prevent enemy microbes from getting a foothold in the body, thus inducing illness or death. When these natural responses do their job in a normal, healthy body, major problems need not occur.

Primary Protection. Great numbers of harmful bacteria exist in the air around us and on our skin. Most of them cannot invade the body, however, because the skin and linings of the gastrointestinal tract serve as a first line of defense against them. Barring injury to these protective shields, we can "swim" through the biotic sea unmolested. Invaders that do enter the body are further subjected to attack by enzymes and acids contained in saliva and stomach secretions.

The Combative Response. What happens when the skin is punctured? Should a splinter, for example, break into the skin of your finger, your body immediately mobilizes tissue cells and white blood cells. The tissue cells surround the particulate matter and engulf it, releasing a barrage of destructive chemicals against the splinter. Simultaneously, millions of white blood cells migrate through the blood-vessel walls and eat the foreign substance, especially bacteria. Thus, most intruding organisms discover a hostile environment within the human body.

The Inflammatory Response. While the tissue cells and white blood cells begin the fight against an invader, the brain soon calls the entire body to help. The small blood vessels expand to allow more blood to flow to the injury. Clear fluids fill the area to dilute any harmful substances. White blood corpuscles are dispatched to the breach in great quantities. Dead cells, killed in battle, along with the white blood cells form pus. Inflamed areas become reddened and give off heat, swelling and pain. We don't understand precisely why pain appears, but we do know that it signals the onset of the healing process. Thus, even though it causes discomfort, it represents a positive response.

The Immune Response. A remarkable event develops within the human body when many harmful bacteria types attack it. Biologists call it the immune response. They explain it by this analogy: A suspicious looking criminal shows up in town. Just before he sets off a crime spree, the police arrest him and throw him in jail. (The criminal is the antigen and the police are called the antibodies.) In this manner, the body prevents a crime wave, and secures itself against future invasion. This analogy describes the immune response in a simple way.

Two important qualities in the human body which provide for the immune response are specificity and memory. Specificity means that only a certain kind of police can arrest a certain kind of criminal. In other words, an antigen can only be stopped by a specific antibody. Memory means that the body remembers the criminal, perhaps by some sort of elaborate "fingerprinting" scheme, and sends out the right kind of police each time he comes to town. The discovery of these qualities formed the basis for inoculation shots. They also help us to understand why certain childhood diseases never return.

Repair and Regeneration

What Happens When the Body Is Injured? When an individual sustains an injury, the human body begins to repair itself and regenerate the damaged or lost tissue. God gave us some cells, like those in the bone marrow and skin, that reproduce themselves continually throughout life. Other cells, like the ones found in the glands and kidney linings, have the capacity to reproduce themselves when they suffer loss. A third kind of cell, called permanent cells, cannot reproduce. Our brain, heart muscles and bones are comprised of these cells.

Most minor injuries affect the skin. God demonstrated His great wisdom, then, by creating the skin cells to reproduce so quickly and easily. Internal injuries that damage the glands can heal too, but more slowly and by greatly restricting the person's activities and lifestyle. The permanent cells of the brain can never be replaced, barring a divine miracle. Brain cells die every day, but the sheer number of them ensures that a sufficient quantity remains to support life. The heart cells cannot regenerate either. After a heart attack, however, scar tissue fills the damaged area. This tissue does not act like the heart muscle, but it enables the rest of the heart to function, if only at a reduced level. Most importantly, life can go on after a heart attack.

Since the majority of minor injuries involve the skin, let's summarize the steps of the skin's healing process. To simplify this description, we will assume that, aside from the injury, this person is healthy. His/her body should respond quickly to the threat.

1. The injured area becomes reddened, swollen and painful, due to the inflammatory response.
2. Blood clotting begins, stopping the bleeding, and forms a scab over the wound.
3. The cells next to the wound start dividing and growing over the injured area.
4. In a minor injury, the replaced skin will be so complete than no permanent markings will result.
5. If the injury is more serious and breaks the skin surface, connective tissue, known as *fibroblasts* spread and fill the wound. These are scar tissue cells, comprised of *fibrils* that are tough and very strong. They lack the characteristics of the skin they replace. They are not as flexible, are less sensitive, and are missing other features such as hair and sweat glands.
6. Irreversible scarring occurs.

Interrelationship of Body Functions. Because of their implications for spiritual healing, it is significant to note how physical healing processes interact in the body. In the normal state, the systems of the entire body work together to maintain health. For example, should the kidneys stop functioning normally, the sodium content of the blood may rise. As a result, the body suffers from high blood pressure. Coupled with stress, this may bring on heart failure. When one system runs into trouble or shuts down, other systems are affected and complications occur quickly.

Diet content profoundly affects the total physical being. We cannot eat simply what tastes good, without regard to the nutritional value in the food, calories, fats, sodium and a host of other substances. Sometimes, the same food may be fine for one person, but toxic to another who has a particular allergy. This reaction explains the use of the terms, for example, of *lactose-intolerant* or *gluten-free*. Not only does diet impact our bodies, we must also carefully monitor temperature, humidity, exercise, stress, rest, exposure to the sun, air quality and anything else that involves our basic survival. Each element affects one or more systems in the body. Each system, in turn, affects the other systems. Eventually, the entire body gets involved.

Similarly, to treat one body system, health care professionals must monitor the direct or side effects on other systems. Hormone replacement therapy, for example, may stop or delay osteoporosis, or deterioration of the bone, but may induce cancer or cause other serious problems. All the body's systems, therefore, must be kept in balance and treatment of one system must not interfere with the operation of another.

Spiritual Healing

Process

Using the process of physical healing as our model, it is clear that the spiritual healing also follows a process. The basic steps of this process are detailed in the following section, "The Eight Steps To Spiritual Healing." Complete, inner healing involves many events which occur systematically, and work interdependently with each other. Physically, should the body not achieve all of the four lines of defense, or should it repel the infection but fail to supply scar tissue or to coagulate the blood, or should it lose the proper balance of the contributing systems, the person will not attain full health. In spiritual healing, one may realize some initial steps toward full salvation, but if he/she falters, or stops along the way, or goes off in another direction, the goal of spiritual health will remain unreached.

> "Blessed is the man whose strength is in You, whose heart is set on pilgrimage. As they pass through the Valley of Baca, they make it a spring; the rain also covers it with pools. They go from strength to strength; each one appears before God in Zion." PSALM 84:5-7

> "And we, who with unveiled faces all reflect the Lord's glory, are being transformed into his likeness with ever-increasing glory, which comes from the Lord, who is the Spirit." II CORINTHIANS 3:8 NIV

In a process, each step builds upon the preceding one. Omitting a step interrupts the process, and negates the end result. Faith without repentance, repentance without water baptism, accepting Christ without obeying His Word, and so on, will leave a candidate for salvation short of the intended goal. There is no hypothetical, absolute bottom line that "faith" does it all, or that infant baptism qualifies as the sole requirement for salvation, or that some other act alone saves anyone. There are no exclusive steps in the quest to be saved. Our observation of the physical healing process clearly shows that no single step is exclusive and independent. Each step works with other steps to form a process. Therefore, it is the process that leads us to the end result of spiritual healing.

Balance

No particular step, by itself, incorporates everything necessary for complete healing. The key lies in **balance**. We must not become so obsessed with any individual step, whether it is faith, repentance, water baptism, or even the baptism of the Holy Spirit, that we feel satisfied with an incomplete healing. This leads to an imbalanced view of full salvation. At each point along the way, a person will feel better. As we will see in a following section, faith does make a person feel better. Repentance makes one feel better. The same may be said for water baptism, prayer, Bible reading, joining a church, listening to a sermon, worshipping God, or any number of spiritual activities. Some mistake these feelings for the ultimate, intended goal, however, and go no further. Sooner or later, they lapse back into sickness.

Medical researchers have proven that an imbalanced diet causes major problems in the human body. Lay persons often think that if a certain food, vitamin or mineral is good for them, then more of it will even be better. Thus, they often overdose on a good thing. On the other hand, they may think that if something seems to have little importance, it can be left out altogether. Not true. Certain chemicals that exist in traces in the body are necessary and good. Whenever those same chemicals get too large in quantity, however, they become lethal. Instead of helping the body, they can actually kill it. If those same chemicals get totally eliminated from the body, however, sickness or even death can occur.

Spiritually, we must not overdose on—nor eliminate—any element of the salvation process. In the church body, for example, there are times when pastors need to concentrate on one thing, whether it be faith, repentance, baptism, worship, holiness, etc. These areas are handled just long enough until the body gets brought back into line. After the body achieves balance, they attend to other needs.

Water baptism is often targeted as unnecessary by some who attempt to "streamline" salvation. To them, it seems to be merely an outward show with no real, eternal or spiritual significance. No one can read very far in the Acts of the Apostles, however, without noting the emphasis that the early church placed upon baptism. It is quite evident that it was important to Jesus because He commanded the first disciples to practice it. Yet, we cannot make so much of water baptism that it becomes the exclusive step to salvation. The point is simply that we must neither eliminate nor overemphasize any step. Everything must be kept in balance.

Equilibrium

Health is not simply a matter of "feeling good." Almost anything—drugs, alcohol, or even emotional euphoria—can temporarily fool the body or the mind into this state. True health requires that the body achieve a state of equilibrium. This important principle in health maintenance holds that the body's resistance must remain at a level high enough to ward off all attackers. While we cannot live in a vacuum where every menacing cell has been removed, we can overcome the harmful effects of hostile cells through healthful living.

Similarly, spiritual health thrives within a right relationship with God. When one finds peace and acceptance with God, He confers an enduring peace that resists all attempts of the world or the devil to interrupt. In other words, the spiritual healthy person maintains an equilibrium with the hostile world around him/her. While the believer may not vanquish sin and Satan from the earth, these enemies of the soul may be kept at bay. Jesus said it best.

> *"Peace I leave with you; my peace I give you. I do not give to you as the world gives. Do not let your hearts be troubled and do not be afraid."* JOHN 14:27

Spiritual healing is a miraculous process, but it is still a process. Sometimes it happens with incredible speed. Rejoicing breaks out in the church when someone is quickly saved, or when someone takes overt, public steps toward salvation. Covert, internal steps are just as vital, although they may not draw as much attention or stir as many hearts. Each step elevates a person's spiritual health and makes the next step accessible.

The Eight Steps to Spiritual Healing

Close observation of salvation allows us to isolate eight steps to spiritual healing. We could also call these the eight confessions of the sinner. They stand out as vital personal revelations to one's journey from spiritual sickness to the spiritual cure. Everyone must traverse through each one of the following steps.

1. "I am sick."   = Repentance
2. "Nothing is working."   = Renunciation
3. "My sickness is terminal."   = Reality Adjustment
4. "There is a cure."   = Recognition
5. "I can be cured."   = Receptivity
6. "I will accept the cure."   = Regeneration
7. "I will follow through with the cure."   = Reconciliation
8. "I will live in spiritual health."   = Responsible Living

The number eight possesses nothing magical. Some scriptural significance may lie in that the number eight is often used in the Bible to set forth a new order of things. For the purpose at hand, eight steps simply seem logical in moving toward spiritual healing. An analysis of actual cases in the lives of many people makes this evident. While scriptural terms exist to describe each step, it helps to see salvation in the context of healing. Every candidate for salvation from sin must come to these points of admission. Since each one constitutes a profoundly spiritual act, we may refer to these admissions as confessions.

First Confession: "I Am Sick."

It has been said that there are two greatest things that a man can know. The first is to know that he is a sinner. The second is to know he is saved. The second is impossible to know without the first. When people admit that they are spiritually sick, it indicates that they have worked through denial. Nothing good starts to happen until a person admits sin.

> "Now we know that whatever the law says, it says to those who are under the law, that every mouth may be stopped, and all the world may become guilty before God. Therefore by the deeds of the law no flesh will be justified in His sight, for by the law is the knowledge of sin.
>
> But now the righteousness of God apart from the law is revealed, being witnessed by the Law and the Prophets, even the righteousness of God, through faith in Jesus Christ, to all and on all who believe. For there is no difference; for all have sinned and fall short of the glory of God." ROMANS 3:19-23

Confession of sin and repentance signal the move to God's grace and favor. They deliver a deathblow to pride. They bring a person out of the fog of half-truths, speculation, human reasoning and lies into spiritual reality and truth. They put one into right perspective in terms of eternity and the Judge of All the Earth. They give a concrete definition to life and death, divinity and humanity, and heaven and earth. Unless a person says, "I am sick," he/she is both unable and unqualified to deal with anything else on a spiritual level.

> "He who covers his sins will not prosper, But whoever confesses and forsakes them will have mercy." PROVERBS 28:13

Survey this list of confessions of men of the Bible. They did not make excuses for themselves. They did not justify their wrongdoing. God's brilliant and revealing light exposed their sin. They knew that open confession was the only way to reconciliation with the Almighty.

> "Then Saul said to Samuel, 'I have sinned, for I have transgressed the commandment of the LORD and your words, because I feared the people and obeyed their voice.'" 1 SAMUEL 15:24

> "So David said to Nathan, 'I have sinned against the LORD.'

And Nathan said to David, 'The LORD also has put away your sin; you shall not die.'" 2 SAMUEL 12:13

"So I said: 'Woe is me, for I am undone! Because I am a man of unclean lips, And I dwell in the midst of a people of unclean lips; For my eyes have seen the King, The LORD of hosts.'" ISAIAH 6:5

"Have mercy upon me, O God, according to Your lovingkindness; according to the multitude of Your tender mercies, blot out my transgressions. Wash me thoroughly from my iniquity, and cleanse me from my sin. For I acknowledge my transgressions, and my sin is always before me. Against You, You only, have I sinned, and done this evil in Your sight—that You may be found just when You speak, and blameless when You judge. Behold, I was brought forth in iniquity, and in sin my mother conceived me." PSALM 51:1-5

"When Simon Peter saw it, he fell down at Jesus' knees, saying, 'Depart from me, for I am a sinful man, O Lord!'" LUKE 5:8

"I will arise and go to my father, and will say to him, 'Father, I have sinned against heaven and before you.'" LUKE 15:18

"This is a faithful saying and worthy of all acceptance, that Christ Jesus came into the world to save sinners, of whom I am chief." 1 TIMOTHY 1:15

Second Confession: "Nothing Is Working."

The second step to spiritual healing is to renounce every other answer to the sickness as a false cure. If another cure to sin existed in the universe, God's sacrifice for sin would have been in vain. Only the blood of Jesus will suffice. Yet, there appear to be many other means. A person must deal directly with these pseudo-cures, and say no to them all. Neither alcohol, drugs, carnal pleasure, wealth, position, possessions, novelties, the occult, wrong relationships nor any other substitute for true salvation will permanently erase the pain of sin.

A person who desires the true cure may confront some of these false cures with great difficulty. "Just say no" is easy to say, but hard to do. Alcohol and drugs cause extreme addiction. Carnal pleasures tempt the flesh severely. False religions sink their roots deeply into one's heritage. Many habits resist change regardless of how heroic the efforts are to break them.

One of the miracles Jesus performed involved a woman with severe hemorrhaging problem. When the opportunity finally appeared for her to find her healing in Christ, she had already spent twelve years seeking a cure from physicians with no results.

> "Now a woman, having a flow of blood for twelve years, who had spent all her livelihood on physicians and could not be healed by any, came from behind and touched the border of His garment. And immediately her flow of blood stopped." LUKE 8:43-44

From a spiritual standpoint, relief from the pain of sin cannot come from any source other than Christ. Anyone who tries an eclectic approach and attempts to take the best of all worlds faces certain failure. The blood of Calvary cannot be mixed together with the wisdom of the world. Many fall into this trap because it plays into the process of human reasoning. It seems wise to try a little bit of everything. Only a total renunciation of all this world's feeble efforts to find an eternal cure, however, will satisfy Christ. To put it plainly, the sinner must confess that nothing else has worked or will work to take away sin or the effects of sin.

Alcohol has not worked.

Drugs have not worked.

Wild living has not worked.

Materialism has not worked.

Education has not worked.

Friends have not worked.

Philosophies and ideas have not worked.

> "Nor is there salvation in any other, for there is no other name under heaven given among men by which we must be saved." ACTS 4:12

Not only do attempts to find a cure to sin outside of Christ fail, they impede the true cure from moving forward in one's life. Physically, as long as the body is simply fighting infection, healing cannot progress. When the infectious agent is driven out, however, repair and regeneration can take place. Spiritually, deep and genuine repentance cuts out the infectious agent of sin. Christ did not come to save us in our sin. He came to save us from our sin. The deeper the repentance, the deeper the cure.

Third Confession: "My Sickness Is Terminal."

Once a sinner confesses that nothing works, he/she must come to terms with sin's prognosis. Sin is not trivial. It is deadly. A vital sense of urgency must grip the sinner. A true cure transcends matters of a slight improvement, a better quality of life, a preferred choice, or even a superior lifestyle. Salvation goes beyond merely suppressing pain. Eternal survival weighs in the balance.

When a doctor diagnoses a terminal illness in a person, it necessitates a sober conference. The patient must hear the bad news.

"I'm sorry to tell you this, John, but the tests came back positive. You have a malignancy."

"Cancer?"

"I'm afraid so."

"What am I going to have to do, Doctor?"

"Well, I believe you need surgery. It's successful with many people, but not with everyone. Most survive the surgery itself, but, to be honest, we don't always get all the cancer. We won't know until we get in there and find out."

"What are my chances?"

"Fair. If we can get it all, if you are up to the surgery, if you can stand the chemo or radiation, and if you will change your lifestyle, then we may be able to give you some extra time."

"I don't know. I hate surgery. What kind of time are we talking about if I don't do anything?"

"Three to six months. This particular type of cancer spreads fast. Untreated, nothing stands in its way. I recommend that you at least do something to slow it down."

Nothing jolts a person into reality faster than this kind of news. Several important truths become clear. First, the disease is fatal. Second, the cure involves radical measures. Third, the clock is ticking. Whatever decision is made, it must be made soon. Fourth, the total cure means a change of lifestyle. Last, there are no alternatives. The patient either accepts the cure, or resigns his/her life to the finality of death.

Let's place this in a spiritual setting. While it is important to present the gospel in a positive light, the unsaved person must, nonetheless, understand that the issues of eternal life and death are at stake. Unfortunately, many people and groups have trivialized the gospel in recent times. They have ignored its gravity, and have focused exclusively on its aspects of love, harmony and experiential religion. By failing to mention the enormity of the decision, these new-styled clerics truncate the cure, and offer far less than the New Testament requires for salvation.

Eternal death awaits the unsaved.

> "For the wages of sin is death, but the gift of God is eternal life in Christ Jesus our Lord." ROMANS 6:23

The gospel must not be viewed as simply another alternative for peace. Without the shed blood of Jesus Christ, accepted by faith and applied through obedience to His word, salvation remains an impossibility. This may come across to sinners as stark, even shocking doctrine. Their world overflows with choices, options, and alternatives. They've seen few black and white issues, mostly just shades of gray. Nevertheless, they must undergo an adjustment to God's reality. Sin is terminal. If they "philosophize" about it, they only blunt its impact on their lives. If they deny it, they only lose time. If they treat it nonchalantly, they create a false sense of security. Sooner or later, they must confront it.

> *"Come now, and let us reason together,"* says the LORD, *"Though your sins are like scarlet, they shall be as white as snow; though they are red like crimson, they shall be as wool."*
> ISAIAH 1:18

Fourth Confession: There Is A Cure

When a person receives the news that he/she has contracted a disease, the next question is usually, "Is it treatable?" Unfortunately, the doctor sometimes says "No. To date, we know of nothing to cure your disease." God, of course, can create His own cure, and we thank Him for His many miracles over disease and even death. Medical science, however, must rely on slow, methodical research. In many cases, it is years away from a cure.

The good news is that a cure exists to the most deadly of all diseases, sin. Although this may seem very basic, it is important to bring a person to this level, because this requires the first step toward salvation, the step of faith. *"And without faith it is impossible to please God, because anyone who comes to him must believe that he exists and that he rewards those who earnestly seek him."* HEBREWS 11:6. Faith says, "Jesus Christ died for the sins of the world."

The sinner must see that Jesus Christ is his/her only way to salvation. The following statements about the saving work of Christ ought to come alive in each person's mind and heart.

1. Sin demanded that a ransom be paid for man's salvation.

    "Just as the Son of Man did not come to be served, but to serve, and to give His life a ransom for many." MATTHEW 20:28

    "For there is one God and one Mediator between God and men, the Man Christ Jesus, who gave Himself a ransom for all, to be testified in due time." 1 TIMOTHY 2:5-6

2. The ransom for man's salvation was the price of blood.

    "And according to the law almost all things are purified with blood, and without shedding of blood there is no remission." HEBREWS 9:22

    "But Christ came as High Priest of the good things to come, with the greater and more perfect tabernacle not made with hands, that is, not of this creation. Not with the blood of goats and calves, but with His own blood He entered the Most Holy Place once for all, having obtained eternal redemption. For if the blood of bulls and goats and the ashes of a heifer, sprinkling the unclean, sanctifies for the purifying of the flesh, how much more shall the blood of Christ, who through the eternal Spirit offered Himself without spot to God, cleanse your conscience from dead works to serve the living God?" HEBREWS 9:11-14

3. No one else but Christ was worthy for the sacrifice.

    "Knowing that you were not redeemed with corruptible things, like silver or gold, from your aimless conduct received by tradition from your fathers, but with the precious blood of Christ, as of a lamb without blemish and without spot." 1 PETER 1:18-19

4. Jesus Christ was God who manifested himself in the flesh in order to save fallen man.

    "God was in Christ reconciling the world to Himself, not imputing their trespasses to them, and has committed to us the

word of reconciliation." 2 Corinthians 5:19

"For in Him dwells all the fullness of the Godhead bodily; and you are complete in Him, who is the head of all principality and power." Colossians 2:9-10

"And you, being dead in your trespasses and the uncircumcision of your flesh, He has made alive together with Him, having forgiven you all trespasses, having wiped out the handwriting of requirements that was against us, which was contrary to us. And He has taken it out of the way, having nailed it to the cross." Colossians 2:13-14

5. Jesus Christ has restored man's relationship with God.

"That at that time you were without Christ, being aliens from the commonwealth of Israel and strangers from the covenants of promise, having no hope and without God in the world. But now in Christ Jesus you who once were far off have been brought near by the blood of Christ. For He Himself is our peace, who has made both one, and has broken down the middle wall of separation, having abolished in His flesh the enmity, that is, the law of commandments contained in ordinances, so as to create in Himself one new man from the two, thus making peace, and that He might reconcile them both to God in one body through the cross, thereby putting to death the enmity." Ephesians 2:12-16

6. Christ alone is the way to salvation.

"'Most assuredly, I say to you, he who does not enter the sheepfold by the door, but climbs up some other way, the same is a thief and a robber. Jesus used this illustration, but they did not understand the things which He spoke to them. Then Jesus said to them again, 'Most assuredly, I say to you, I am the door of the sheep.'" John 10:1-2, 6-7

Fifth Confession: I Can Be Cured

Once a person recognizes that the cure for sin rests in Jesus Christ, and in no one or nothing else, the next step suggests itself. It is time to personalize salvation. This step has a counterpart in the realm of physical healing when a diseased person understands that a cure exists, but it looks too complicated, too expensive, too remote or too risky to undertake. Often, the psychological barriers loom as formidable as the physical or medical procedures. Some people cannot muster the ability to identify with wellness or health. They have been sick for so long, or their problem is so great that they talk themselves out of the cure. They know that others have succeeded, but they cannot, or will not, see themselves in that role.

Good things start to happen the moment a sinner activates faith in the Lord Jesus Christ. It compares to the seed which drops into fertile, moist ground. The life in the seed breaks forth, and sends tiny roots into the soil around it. Soon, a tender stem pokes through the ground to be greeted by the warm sun and cool rain. Likewise, faith generates a chain of healing, curative effects. There are many critical events that must follow this new beginning, but nothing happens until one personally proclaims, "I can be cured!"

Consider the following reasons why many people never take this step from recognition to receptivity. These ideas will not allow them to cross the bridge from recognizing that a cure exists to receiving that cure for themselves.

"God could never love me."

"I am worthless."

"My sins are too great."

"I will just fail again, like everything else I've tried."

"I've tried praying before. It doesn't work for me."

"I have offended God. He won't listen to me."

Satan delights in deceiving people with these falsehoods. None of them stand up, however, in the light of the Word of God.

1. God loves each individual person.

    "But God demonstrates His own love toward us, in that while we were still sinners, Christ died for us." ROMANS 5:8

    "For God so loved the world that He gave His only begotten Son, that whoever believes in Him should not perish but have everlasting life." JOHN 3:16

2. Each person is worth the whole world.

    "So God created man in His own image; in the image of God He created him; male and female He created them." GENESIS 1:27

    "For what profit is it to a man if he gains the whole world, and loses his own soul? Or what will a man give in exchange for his soul?" MATTHEW 16:26

3. No sin is too great for God to forgive.

    "For if when we were enemies we were reconciled to God through the death of His Son, much more, having been reconciled, we shall be saved by His life." ROMANS 5:10

    "Do you not know that the unrighteous will not inherit the kingdom of God? Do not be deceived. Neither fornicators, nor idolaters, nor adulterers, nor homosexuals, nor sodomites, nor thieves, nor covetous, nor drunkards, nor revilers, nor extortioners will inherit the kingdom of God. And such were some of you. But you were washed, but you were sanctified, but you were justified in the name of the Lord Jesus and by the Spirit of our God." 1 CORINTHIANS 6:9-11

4. Each person must trust in God who never fails.

    "No temptation has overtaken you except such as is common to man; but God is faithful, who will not allow you to

be tempted beyond what you are able, but with the temptation will also make the way of escape, that you may be able to bear it." 1 CORINTHIANS 10:13

"O wretched man that I am! Who will deliver me from this body of death? I thank God—through Jesus Christ our Lord! So then, with the mind I myself serve the law of God, but with the flesh the law of sin." ROMANS 7:24-25

5. When a person prays in faith, God will hear.

"Also He spoke this parable to some who trusted in themselves that they were righteous, and despised others: 'Two men went up to the temple to pray, one a Pharisee and the other a tax collector. The Pharisee stood and prayed thus with himself, 'God, I thank You that I am not like other men—extortioners, unjust, adulterers, or even as this tax collector. I fast twice a week; I give tithes of all that I possess.' And the tax collector, standing afar off, would not so much as raise his eyes to heaven, but beat his breast, saying, 'God, be merciful to me a sinner!' I tell you, this man went down to his house justified rather than the other; for everyone who exalts himself will be humbled, and he who humbles himself will be exalted." LUKE 18:9-14

6. God will not hold men in judgment for offending Him when they turn toward Him in meekness and ask to be saved.

"For if when we were enemies we were reconciled to God through the death of His Son, much more, having been reconciled, we shall be saved by His life. And not only that, but we also rejoice in God through our Lord Jesus Christ, through whom we have now received the reconciliation." ROMANS 5:10-11

Sixth Confession: I Will Accept the Cure

The story of Naaman sheds much light on the sixth step, "I will accept the cure." Naaman was a military commander for the king of Syria. He was great in every regard, except he had leprosy. One day, one of his servant maidens, a Hebrew, told him of the prophet Elisha in Samaria who could heal him of his leprosy. Naaman journeyed to Elisha's door bearing many precious gifts, and asked for healing. Elisha, in Naaman's opinion, treated him coarsely. Without bothering to come to the door, Elisha sent word to Naaman to go and wash in the Jordan River.

> "And Elisha sent a messenger to him, saying, 'Go and wash in the Jordan seven times, and your flesh shall be restored to you, and you shall be clean.' But Naaman became furious, and went away and said, 'Indeed, I said to myself, 'He will surely come out to me, and stand and call on the name of the LORD his God, and wave his hand over the place, and heal the leprosy. Are not the Abanah and the Pharpar, the rivers of Damascus, better than all the waters of Israel? Could I not wash in them and be clean?' So he turned and went away in a rage." KINGS 5:10-12

You can see how Naaman had taken each of the steps to this point. He confessed his sickness; he knew nothing else would work; he knew his disease was terminal; he understood that there was a cure; and he personally confessed that this cure could be his. Now, a huge obstacle rose in front of him. He disdained the procedure by which he was to appropriate the cure. He saw dipping in the Jordan River degrading and insulting.

In his rage, Naaman acted irrationally. He began to compare the rivers back home to the Jordan, as though the healing virtue was in the water itself. He evidently felt that leprosy was better than the preposterous cure Elisha proposed, and was willing to go home a leper with the illusion of honor than to go home cured with real honor. His servants saw through his thinly disguised pride.

> "And his servants came near and spoke to him, and said, 'My father, if the prophet had told you to do something great,

would you not have done it? How much more then, when he says to you, 'Wash, and be clean'?" KINGS 5:13

Because of pride and anger, Naaman nearly missed his only chance for healing. He had done everything but accept the actual cure that was offered to him. Regeneration can only begin when the sinner embraces the full cure. The full cure begins in the heart and mind. It must find expression from a person's mouth.

> "But the righteousness of faith speaks in this way, 'Do not say in your heart, 'Who will ascend into heaven?' (that is, to bring Christ down from above) or, 'Who will descend into the abyss?' " (that is, to bring Christ up from the dead). But what does it say? 'The word is near you, in your mouth and in your heart' (that is, the word of faith which we preach): that if you confess with your mouth the Lord Jesus and believe in your heart that God has raised Him from the dead, you will be saved. For with the heart one believes unto righteousness, and with the mouth confession is made unto salvation." ROMANS 10:6-10

So what did Naaman do? He swallowed his pride and simply did what the prophet told him to do. No one should confuse this with "earning salvation", or getting saved by works. Nothing Naaman did glorified him or brought accolades to him for mighty feats. He simply obeyed the voice of the prophet.

> "So he went down and dipped seven times in the Jordan, according to the saying of the man of God; and his flesh was restored like the flesh of a little child, and he was clean." 2 KINGS 5:14.

What does Jesus Christ require for salvation today? Naaman's experience serves as a model for the proper attitude, but his cure applied only to leprosy. How can we, in our generation, be cleansed from our sin? Jesus had some forceful words that addressed this matter in the New Testament.

> "There was a man of the Pharisees named Nicodemus, a

> ruler of the Jews. This man came to Jesus by night and said to Him, 'Rabbi, we know that You are a teacher come from God; for no one can do these signs that You do unless God is with him.' Jesus answered and said to him, 'Most assuredly, I say to you, unless one is born again, he cannot see the kingdom of God.' Nicodemus said to Him, 'How can a man be born when he is old? Can he enter a second time into his mother's womb and be born?' Jesus answered, "Most assuredly, I say to you, unless one is born of water and the Spirit, he cannot enter the kingdom of God.'" JOHN 3:1-5

Do not stop short of this step. Do not stand on the sidelines of the gospel (as it were) and nod affirmatively. Faith must not be defined as only a condition of one's heart that, when God observes it, He perfunctorily grants salvation. True belief leads to action. Faith and obedience go hand in hand. A person can measure faith by the extent of obedience to the Word of God in his/her life. The faith that saves is the faith that obeys.

> "Now to Him who is able to establish you according to my gospel and the preaching of Jesus Christ, according to the revelation of the mystery kept secret since the world began but now has been made manifest, and by the prophetic Scriptures has been made known to all nations, according to the commandment of the everlasting God, for obedience to the faith." ROMANS 16:25-26

When Jesus left this earth, he gave the task of reaching the world and preaching the gospel to His church. He personally selected the group of people who would begin to carry out this gigantic mission. Their inaugural service took place on the Day of Pentecost when the Holy Spirit fell on them. This created a great spectacle and attracted a crowd at an opportune time. Jerusalem was filled with Jewish celebrants of the Feast of Pentecost.

> "When the Day of Pentecost had fully come, they were all with one accord in one place. And suddenly there came a sound from

heaven, as of a rushing mighty wind, and it filled the whole house where they were sitting. Then there appeared to them divided tongues, as of fire, and one sat upon each of them. And they were all filled with the Holy Spirit and began to speak with other tongues, as the Spirit gave them utterance." ACTS 2:1-4

When the crowd came running, Peter, the spokesman, stood up and began to preach about Jesus Christ. His stinging words cut deep into the hearts of those who had recently crucified Christ.

"Now when they heard this, they were cut to the heart, and said to Peter and the rest of the apostles, 'Men and brethren, what shall we do?'" ACTS 2:37

Again, Peter seized the moment. His words fulfilled the earlier instructions of Christ to Nicodemus. He explained what it meant to be born of the water and spirit.

"Then Peter said to them, 'Repent, and let every one of you be baptized in the name of Jesus Christ for the remission of sins; and you shall receive the gift of the Holy Spirit. For the promise is to you and to your children, and to all who are afar off, as many as the Lord our God will call.' And with many other words he testified and exhorted them, saying, 'Be saved from this perverse generation.' Then those who gladly received his word were baptized; and that day about three thousand souls were added to them." ACTS 2:38-41

This cure was shocking to this Jewish crowd. Peter demanded that they admit their crime against Christ and, instead of rejecting Him, he ordered them to *be baptized in His name!* These instructions were far more insulting and bitter to them than was Elisha's command to Naaman. To accept Christ openly and publicly, meant to affirm all that Christ did and taught. They had vehemently opposed these miracles and doctrines for over three years. Yet, this was their only means to salvation.

In medical practice, a similar scenario unfolds. The diagnostic physician lays out a critical situation to a patient. He/she then proceeds to outline several routes to a cure. In especially bad cases, the doctor may recommend radical surgery, amputation of a limb or an organ transplant. In oncology, chemotherapy and radiation are often prescribed. With each measure, the risks become greater and the danger of negative side effects increases. Patients often get so frightened at the cure that they elect to do nothing. The disease seems better than the remedy.

At this juncture, many patients go out to seek a second or third opinion. Before submitting to a radical cure, they run the problem by other doctors, hoping that one of them will have more pleasant news for them. The range of answers they receive is limited only by the number of doctors they see. They often become confused by the differing opinions of several medical doctors. Moreover, many people add to their confusion by talking to those in the "twilight zone" of medicine—adherents of acupuncture, herbal therapies, hypnosis and psychic practitioners.

Spiritually, the victim of sin must embrace the full, scriptural cure for sin. Salvation may appear radical, but it is the only viable remedy. To search for a second opinion only wastes time. Many self-styled healers proclaim every kind of cure imaginable. In the end, however, the serious person who wants to be saved treks back to the Lord Jesus Christ and His gospel.

Seventh Confession: I Will Follow Through With the Cure

Every step in this process is vital, but if one step could be classified as the most crucial, this one is it. Good intentions, promises and words either gain or lose credibility at this step. Often, savvy people quickly learn what they are expected to say, and say it to give the appearance of cooperation. Even sincere people who know they need to change their lives sail smoothly along until they reach this point. This step tests commitments, tries faith and examines the sincerity of a person's intentions. Once a person knows what to do, it becomes his/her responsibility to do it. Only by following through with our intentions do we achieve full reconciliation with God.

Follow-through ensures that thoughts become realities, that ideas become facts. The records of hospitals and surgeons reveal the number of "no-shows," or people who were scheduled for surgery but didn't keep their appointments. Even more common is the number of people who fail to keep their doctor's orders, who do not take regularly prescribed medicine or who "cheat" on diets and exercise programs. No one can claim ignorance of the cure at this point. The problem lies with the character of the one who is sick.

Spiritually, the lack of follow-through presents a major stumbling block to many people. James says,

> "But be doers of the word, and not hearers only, deceiving yourselves. For if anyone is a hearer of the word and not a doer, he is like a man observing his natural face in a mirror; for he observes himself, goes away, and immediately forgets what kind of man he was. But he who looks into the perfect law of liberty and continues in it, and is not a forgetful hearer but a doer of the work, this one will be blessed in what he does." JAMES 1:22-25

The success of any cure depends upon the actual, physical, real-life follow-through. The cure does not exist in the laboratory vials or test tubes. It does not exist in the volumes of reports, test results or conferences. It does not exist in the x-rays or ultra-sound videos or computer printouts. All these are preliminary to the application of the cure. Nothing happens until the patient is wheeled into the surgical suite.

Unfortunately, many people who seek a cure for their spiritual pain bog down in the preliminary procedures. To them, the cure exists in their minds or on paper, but they do not follow through. All they end up with is an illusion, even though that illusion may be logically thought out and may have all the earmarks of a cure. It is not a cure until it is fully applied.

The greatest example of follow-through is our Lord Himself. With one word, He could have effected salvation for everyone. One wave of His hand could have destroyed Satan. Calvary could have been virtual. One thought arcing across his mind could have washed sin from the world. Yet, He entered the world in the form of a man, and died an actual death on the cross for us. He did not turn His faith into a "mind cult." He did not retain His Word on an intellectual, ethereal plane.

> *"The Word became flesh and made his dwelling among us."*
> JOHN 1:14

The foregoing paragraph has historical precedent. The Apostle John combated a group of heretics called Gnostics who denied that Jesus came in the flesh. They placed such value on the mental plane that they believed the fleshly existence was too evil for Christ to enter. Of this error, John wrote, *"Beloved, do not believe every spirit, but test the spirits, whether they are of God; because many false prophets have gone out into the world. By this you know the Spirit of God: Every spirit that confesses that Jesus Christ has come in the flesh is of God, and every spirit that does not confess that Jesus Christ has come in the flesh is not of God. And this is the spirit of the Antichrist, which you have heard was coming, and is now already in the world."* JOHN 4:1-3.

The Apostle Paul also stressed the importance of physically involving our whole being in our relationship with God.

> *"I beseech you therefore, brethren, by the mercies of God, that you present your bodies a living sacrifice, holy, acceptable to God, which is your reasonable service. And do not be conformed to this world, but be transformed by the renewing of your mind, that you may prove what is that good and acceptable and perfect will of God."* ROMANS 12:1-2

Follow through with faith. Faith is a starting point, not an end in itself. Faith works as a vehicle to take a person to a spiritual destination. When one truly believes something, he/she will act upon those beliefs.

Follow through with repentance. Repentance reflects changes in the intellect, emotions and will. Intellectually, we must understand that sin is wrong and an offense against God. Emotionally, we must feel sorrow for sin. Then, we must act willfully to turn away from sin. If one continues in sin, true repentance has not taken place.

Follow through with water baptism. The normative New Testament pattern for salvation incorporated water baptism for each candidate. Both Peter and Paul stressed this step in their ministries.

> *"While Peter was still speaking these words, the Holy Spirit fell upon all those who heard the word. And those of the circumcision who believed were astonished, as many as came with Peter, because the gift of the Holy Spirit had been poured out on the Gentiles also. For they heard them speak with tongues and magnify God. Then Peter answered, 'Can anyone forbid water, that these should not be baptized who have received the Holy Spirit just as we have?' And he commanded them to be baptized in the name of the Lord. Then they asked him to stay a few days."* ACTS 10:44-48

> *"And it happened, while Apollos was at Corinth, that Paul, having passed through the upper regions, came to Ephesus. And finding some disciples he said to them, 'Did you receive the Holy Spirit when you believed?' So they said to him, 'We have not so much as heard whether there is a Holy Spirit.' And he said to them, 'Into what then were you baptized?' So they said, 'Into John's baptism.' Then Paul said, 'John indeed baptized with a baptism of repentance, saying to the people that they should believe on Him who would come after him, that is, on Christ Jesus.' When they heard this, they were baptized in the name of the Lord Jesus."* ACTS 19:1-5

Follow through with the Spirit baptism. The new birth

experience remains incomplete until birth comes by both water and Spirit. Jesus told His disciples to wait in the city of Jerusalem until they had received the Spirit, or "power from on high." He knew that their mission in this world would fail without sufficient spiritual power. He insisted that they get this power.

> "And being assembled together with them, He commanded them not to depart from Jerusalem, but to wait for the Promise of the Father, 'which,' He said, 'you have heard from Me; for John truly baptized with water, but you shall be baptized with the Holy Spirit not many days from now.'" ACTS 1:4-5

> "But you shall receive power when the Holy Spirit has come upon you; and you shall be witnesses to Me in Jerusalem, and in all Judea and Samaria, and to the end of the earth." ACTS 1:8

In strict obedience to the words of Jesus, the disciples returned to Jerusalem to wait for the Holy Spirit. After ten days, their patience paid off.

> "And they were all filled with the Holy Spirit and began to speak with other tongues, as the Spirit gave them utterance." ACTS 2:4

The Apostle Peter did not restrict this experience to this initial outpouring on the disciples in the upper room. He threw open the doors widely to all who would listen.

> "For the promise is to you and to your children, and to all who are afar off, as many as the Lord our God will call." ACTS 2:38-39

Follow through with discipleship. Physically, it would be foolish to cure a cancer without an attempt to restore the body to full health. Spiritually, full, sacrificial discipleship stands at apex of living the saved life. Jesus said, *"If anyone desires to come after Me, let him deny himself, and take up his cross daily, and follow Me. For whoever desires to save his life will lose it, but whoever loses his life for*

My sake will save it." LUKE 9:23-24.

Again, it would be foolish to cure a cancer without teaching the patient how to prevent its recurrence. Without discipleship, there can be no relationship. We must be "in Christ." Our salvation rests in this relationship with Christ. A signed card on file in the church office, or a superficial prayer at the close of an evangelistic service is no more a relationship with Christ than a marriage certificate is a marriage. Discipleship demands follow-through.

Eighth Confession: I Will Live In Spiritual Health

Two major factors shape an individual's health. One can be controlled; the other cannot. The factor which defies control is comprised of elements such as genetic diseases, congenital allergies and conditions, unknown environmental factors, accidents and unavoidable injuries. The other factor lies in the realm of the individual's control. Each person decides what to eat, what to drink, whether or not to smoke, whether or not to engage in hazardous occupations or activities, and makes other choices that impinge upon his/her health.

Often, people who seemed to be in the pink of health have collapsed and died because of an internal condition they knew nothing about. Others who were obviously healthy have destroyed their own lives as a result of either foolish or calculated risks. One may not be able to avoid traffic accidents in normal, responsible driving, but choosing to drag race or to drive recklessly is another matter. A person may not be responsible for a congenital heart defect, but should he/she smoke, drink liquor, use narcotics, overdose on sugar and sodium, and eat fatty foods, then the blame for poor health or premature death cannot be assigned to fate or ignorance.

This comparison leads us to the final confession, "I will live in spiritual health." Remembering that spiritual healing lies in process, balance and equilibrium, we can readily see the importance of responsible living. While a person cannot control every threat to his/

her health, those forces which can be controlled, ought to be. Each person must accept some responsibility for life.

This need for spiritually responsible living does not negate the grace of God in our lives any more than a healthy diet takes the place of a good set of genes. God has abundantly taken care of His part by granting us a new heart. *"I will give you a new heart and put a new spirit within you; I will take the heart of stone out of your flesh and give you a heart of flesh. I will put My Spirit within you and cause you to walk in My statutes, and you will keep My judgments and do them."* EZEKIEL 36:26-27. This profound spiritual change places us in a new realm. No force has power over us any more to destroy us.

> *"What then shall we say to these things? If God is for us, who can be against us? He who did not spare His own Son, but delivered Him up for us all, how shall He not with Him also freely give us all things? Who shall bring a charge against God's elect? It is God who justifies. Who is he who condemns? It is Christ who died, and furthermore is also risen, who is even at the right hand of God, who also makes intercession for us. Who shall separate us from the love of Christ? Shall tribulation, or distress, or persecution, or famine, or nakedness, or peril, or sword? As it is written: 'For Your sake we are killed all day long; We are accounted as sheep for the slaughter.' Yet in all these things we are more than conquerors through Him who loved us. For I am persuaded that neither death nor life, nor angels nor principalities nor powers, nor things present nor things to come, nor height nor depth, nor any other created thing, shall be able to separate us from the love of God which is in Christ Jesus our Lord."* ROMANS 8:31-39

Our spiritual genes are programmed for success. God has carefully positioned us so we may take full advantage of His grace, power and wisdom. But does this act alone absolve us from all responsibility? Let our medical model answer that question. Suppose a person's doctor says, "You have a clean bill of health. Everything checks out in perfect order. I don't see any reason why you should have any restrictions on your life whatsoever." Does this report mean that this same person should abandon a healthy lifestyle on the premise of the doctor's statement? Of course not. Let's see why.

Paul's statement in ROMANS 8:31-39 reflects the power and handiwork of God. In it, the Apostle simply affirms God's intentions for believers, and His divine ability to back up every word of His

The Eight Steps to Spiritual Healing

promises. There is no intent to give us license to break every principle of spiritual health. He established this truth in an earlier chapter.

"What shall we say then? Shall we continue in sin that grace may abound? Certainly not! How shall we who died to sin live any longer in it? Or do you not know that as many of us as were baptized into Christ Jesus were baptized into His death? Therefore we were buried with Him through baptism into death, that just as Christ was raised from the dead by the glory of the Father, even so we also should walk in newness of life." ROMANS 6:1-4

The secret of sustained spiritual health is clear. After a person is saved, he/she must begin to live in a spiritually healthy way. Unless this happens, every advantage of the new birth can be squandered away.

"And you, who once were alienated and enemies in your mind by wicked works, yet now He has reconciled in the body of His flesh through death, to present you holy, and blameless, and above reproach in His sight—if indeed you continue in the faith, grounded and steadfast, and are not moved away from the hope of the gospel which you heard, which was preached to every creature under heaven, of which I, Paul, became a minister." COLOSSIANS 1:21-23

Paul recognized the danger of falling. To the Corinthians, he wrote, *"And everyone who competes for the prize is temperate in all things. Now they do it to obtain a perishable crown, but we for an imperishable crown. Therefore I run thus: not with uncertainty. Thus I fight: not as one who beats the air. But I discipline my body and bring it into subjection, lest, when I have preached to others, I myself should become disqualified."* CORINTHIANS 9:25-27.

Others had not practiced such a disciplined and responsible life. Their lives ended in disaster. Paul exhorts Timothy to avoid their same fate.

> *"This charge I commit to you, son Timothy, according to the prophecies previously made concerning you, that by them you may wage the good warfare, having faith and a good conscience, which some having rejected, concerning the faith have suffered shipwreck, of whom are Hymenaeus and Alexander, whom I delivered to Satan that they may learn not to blaspheme."*
> 1 TIMOTHY 1:18-20

Physical health is not a goal to be reached and then forgotten. It is not a test of one's ability to hit a target. Health is a state of being, a condition to be maintained in the face of adversity and challenge. Health is not the absence of sickness, but proper balance of the body. When injury or infection comes, the healthy body responds appropriately and returns the body to its balanced state.

Spiritual health follows the same pattern. It is bound up in an ongoing relationship with Jesus Christ. This final step makes all the other steps worthwhile. The true objective of Christ in salvation is not only to touch the lives of believers, but also to be involved with them, commune with them and walk with them on a daily basis. Only this fulfills the purpose of redemption.

The Therapeutic Value of Salvation

The word "therapy" is a Greek word which means "healing." It is a popular term today applied to nearly everything from physician-prescribed physical therapy, to relaxation and exercise to exotic medical treatments. Therapy evokes positive feelings. In this final section of our book, let us firmly establish the therapeutic value in each phase of salvation. It for soul winners to see that salvation transcends a set of hard commands to be obeyed, or meaningless rituals that people have to go through before they get to the "good stuff." Each required step of the salvation process contributes profoundly to the inner healing that every soul desperately needs. Sinners must see that Jesus Christ is the way to peace and freedom from pain.

Every move towards God is divinely therapeutic. At the same time, we must keep in mind the principles of process, balance and equilibrium. By extolling the virtues of each step, we are not denying or excluding other steps. Each element plays a valuable part in reaching the ultimate goal of complete spiritual health.

Faith

The moment a person activates faith in Christ, healing virtue is released. A remarkable story took place in the ministry of Christ which demonstrates this fact.

> *"And suddenly, a woman who had a flow of blood for twelve years came from behind and touched the hem of His garment. For she said to herself, 'If only I may touch His garment, I shall be made well.'*
>
> *But Jesus turned around, and when He saw her He said, 'Be of good cheer, daughter; your faith has made you well.' And the woman was made well from that hour."* MATTHEW 9:20-22

While this was an instance of a physical healing, the power of faith itself is the same, whether it heals in a physical or a spiritual sense.

Even the secular world has discovered this power, if only in a limited way. They speak of a "positive mental attitude," autosuggestion, possibility thinking, visualization, the magic of believing, and so on. People can create powerful imagery through the exercise of faith. It can be so forceful that it leads to triumph over formidable odds and helps individuals achieve goals that had never before been possible.

The simple connection between inner healing and faith should excite the soul winner. Any person who suffers from the pain of sin can experience immediate help when he/she starts believing in Christ. This is not to say that embryonic faith constitutes full salvation. Salvation is still a process. But faith in Christ starts the process in motion! Consider these scriptures:

> "Now faith is the substance of things hoped for, the evidence of things not seen."

> "By faith we understand that the worlds were framed by the word of God, so that the things which are seen were not made of things which are visible."

> "But without faith it is impossible to please Him, for he who comes to God must believe that He is, and that He is a rewarder of those who diligently seek Him." HEBREWS 11:1,3,6

People who begin in faith enter into the provincial realm of God's promises. As long as they continue, they will enjoy total spiritual healing.

> "Being confident of this very thing, that He who has begun a good work in you will complete it until the day of Jesus Christ."
> PHILIPPIANS 1:6

Specifically, faith brings healing to a number of sin's injuries. Faith fills the vacuum created by doubt. Faith counteracts the negative influences of fear. Faith reverses one's sense of worthlessness and unimportance. Faith helps build back self-esteem. Faith dispels the clouds of depression. Faith connects the heart and soul with God. Faith pleases God. However faith is considered, it is wholesome, positive and good.

Repentance

Unfortunately, repentance has too often been cast in a negative light, probably because it involves pain and loss. It does represent the bloody sacrifices at the brazen altar, Christ's death on the cross, humiliation, self-denial and a harsh change from a sinful life to holiness. Sometimes it appears so intimidating that many people become discouraged just thinking about it. No one likes pain or loss, and if people have the limited view that this is all repentance means, they will balk at it.

We cannot deny that repentance means death to the flesh. Far more important, however, repentance delivers powerful therapeutic effects. As we emphasize these positive results, we inspire courage and confidence in people to follow through with repentance.

Repentance aligns a person with the true gospel. *"And that repentance and remission of sins should be preached in His name to all nations, beginning at Jerusalem."* LUKE 24:47

Repentance paves the way for the Holy Ghost baptism. *"Peter replied, "Repent and be baptized, every one of you, in the name of Jesus Christ for the forgiveness of your sins. And you will receive the gift of the Holy Spirit."* ACTS 2:38

Repentance is a gift of God. *"When they heard this, they had no further objections and praised God, saying, "So then, God has granted even the Gentiles repentance unto life."* ACTS 11:18

Repentance indicates God's love and good intentions. *"God's kindness leads you toward repentance."* ROMANS 2:4

Repentance leads to reconciliation with God. *"Godly sorrow brings repentance that leads to salvation and leaves no regret, but worldly sorrow brings death."* 2 CORINTHIANS 7:10

Again, let's examine the medical model to gain insight into repentance. The first steps toward the cure of a disease or the healing of an injury involve pain. Dead tissue must be cut away, toxins must be drained from a wound, infections must be attacked by strong antidotes, broken bones must be reset, tourniquets must be applied, and shock therapy must be administered to restart vital signs. Whatever it takes to bring a diseased or injured person back to safe medical grounds must be done, often without regard to the pain that the procedure inflicts.

But the pain caused by the cure differs from that caused by the disease or injury. It is a pain filled with hope. It is meaningful pain. It says, "Smile through the hurt, because you're going to feel better after it's over!" The repentant soul must say, "I give control to the process of healing. I submit to the physician's plan." PROVERBS 27:6 (NIV) says, *"Wounds from a friend can be trusted, but an enemy multiplies kisses."* If repentance symbolizes the crucifixion of Christ, it is good to remember that it is only a symbol. Christ absorbed the full impact of the cross, the penalty for our sins, so that we could be spared from eternal death. Without that supreme act of love, we would have to bear our own penalty. How much better it is to repent than to be crucified!

Repentance heals because it stops the infection of sin in one's heart. Repentance heals because it releases a person from the hold of sin. Repentance heals because it alerts one to the root of spiritual pain. Repentance heals because it establishes a connection with God himself. Repentance heals because it changes a person's perspective of himself/herself. Repentance aligns us with God's true perception of us: redeemed sinners now His children! Repentance heals because it removes the oppressive weight of guilt and other emotional baggage that one has carried around for years. Repentance heals because it sets God free to operate in one's life. Nothing other than complete repentance can bring about such deep and profound positive changes.

Soul winners who lead people to repentance must not hurriedly push them through this process as though it had relatively little meaning. Repentance may precede other important spiritual steps, but it is itself bringing about vital changes that must not be lightly dismissed. Repentance needs to go deep. The soul winner needs to understand and be able to explain to the repenting sinner what is happening. Also, a new convert ought to have time to savor the momentous event taking place in his/her heart.

> "Likewise, I say to you, there is joy in the presence of the angels of God over one sinner who repents." Luke 15:10

Water Baptism

In our discussion of spiritual healing, we referred to the importance of water baptism. Mysteriously, water baptism has almost acquired a stigma among some groups in their effort to stress salvation by faith alone. This unbalanced view amounts to a denial of baptism in some cases. When the subject of water baptism is mentioned, they experience a phobic reaction. In fact, the statement of Jesus, *"He who believes and is baptized will be saved; but he who does not believe will be condemned."* (MARK 16:15) has caused such embarrassment to them that some have blatantly rewritten it to say, "He that believes and is *not* baptized shall be saved." This unscriptural revision has unwittingly locked up the divine therapy that water baptism was meant to convey.

We must not place water baptism over against faith to determine which one is responsible for salvation. Rather, let us unravel the purpose of water baptism and search out the therapeutic value that God intended through it.

Baptism conveys a cleansing experience. Baptism was practiced long before Christ or even John the Baptist. Since baptism is a Greek word, we don't readily recognize it in the Old Testament. Usually, when we see references to "washings" they mean the same thing we understand as baptism in the New Testament. Old covenant believers viewed baptism as signifying spiritual change. Whenever repentance swept across the people, baptism meant a revived relationship towards God. Washings also symbolized ceremonial purification.

New Testament believers should enter into baptism with strong overtones of cleansing and absolution. Corruption and impurity in the soul flee as a person is plunged beneath the baptismal waters. Afterwards, the baptized believer should glow from the experience. Baptism is intended to be a powerful healing agent for the soul.

Baptism is for the remission of sins. According to the scripture, baptism is intrinsic to the remission of sins. Two verses, in particular, highlight this fact:

> *"Then Peter said to them, 'Repent, and let every one of you be baptized in the name of Jesus Christ for the remission of sins; and you shall receive the gift of the Holy Spirit.'"* ACTS 2:38

> *"And now why are you waiting? Arise and be baptized, and wash away your sins, calling on the name of the Lord."* ACTS 22:16

Baptism directly addresses sin in each deleterious aspect. First, it applies healing virtue to damaged emotions. Second, it erases the standing record of sin against the believer. Third, it absolves the soul of guilt. Fourth, it provides an eternal asylum from sin's destructive nature. Fifth, it breaks the connection between the sinner and the past.

We must be careful to mention that the water itself does not cleanse. Neither is there sin remitting power contained in the ceremony itself. Yet, when water baptism is administered in faith, it conveys something spiritual to the candidate.

Baptism joins the believer to Christ. Paul writes to the Galatians, *"For as many of you as were baptized into Christ have put on Christ."* GALATIANS 3:27. Getting into Christ happens through more than an exercise of faith. This scripture points out the role of baptism as the agent. When a believer is baptized, he/she enters into Christ. This provides access to every victory Jesus won for us. His death, burial and resurrection belong to the church. His victory over Satan, the flesh and the world belong to the church. His triumph over sin belongs to the church. Baptism positions us in an unbeatable place.

One of the most important psychological principles for mental and emotional health is the sense of belonging. Baptism places the believer into the family of God, into the body of Christ on earth (the church). We understand that Christ belongs to the church: more significantly, the church belongs to Christ! His victories are ours, our defeats are His. To those who have experienced rejection, hatred or discrimination, this truth heals deep wounds.

> *"For by one Spirit we were all baptized into one body—whether Jews or Greeks, whether slaves or free—and have all been made to drink into one Spirit."* 1 CORINTHIANS 12:13

Baptism also imparts healing to us through the principle of identification. We become identified with Christ in the waters of baptism.

> *"Or do you not know that as many of us as were baptized into Christ Jesus were baptized into His death? Therefore we were buried with Him through baptism into death, that just as Christ was raised from the dead by the glory of the Father, even so we also should walk in newness of life."* ROMANS 6:3-4

Baptism swallows up our marred, corrupt identity. We then become one with Christ.

> *"Therefore, if anyone is in Christ, he is a new creation; old things have passed away; behold, all things have become new."* 2 CORINTHIANS 5:17

Baptism invokes the saving name of Jesus Christ over the believer. A careful reading of the New Testament reveals that the name of Jesus Christ was used exclusively in baptism. Several of these instances have been quoted previously. Here are two more.

> "Who, when they had come down, prayed for them that they might receive the Holy Spirit. For as yet He had fallen upon none of them. They had only been baptized in the name of the Lord Jesus." Acts 8:15-16

> "And he said to them, 'Into what then were you baptized?' So they said, 'Into John's baptism.' Then Paul said, 'John indeed baptized with a baptism of repentance, saying to the people that they should believe on Him who would come after him, that is, on Christ Jesus.' When they heard this, they were baptized in the name of the Lord Jesus." Acts 19:3-5

The use of the name of Jesus is highly significant, especially in terms of the healing of the soul. God always manifested His power on earth through the use of His name.

The name of Jesus confers salvation. "*Nor is there salvation in any other, for there is no other name under heaven given among men by which we must be saved.*" ACTS 4:12

The name of Jesus puts devils to flight. "*And this she did for many days. But Paul, greatly annoyed, turned and said to the spirit, 'I command you in the name of Jesus Christ to come out of her.' And he came out that very hour.*" ACTS 16:18

The name of Jesus holds power over physical ailments. "*Then Peter said, 'Silver and gold I do not have, but what I do have I give you: In the name of Jesus Christ of Nazareth, rise up and walk.' And he took him by the right hand and lifted him up, and immediately his feet and ankle bones received strength. So he, leaping up, stood and walked and entered the temple with them--walking, leaping, and praising God.*" ACTS 3:6-8

Baptism places within our grasp the use of the name of Jesus. The very name which wielded so much power in the early church belongs to baptized believers. The therapeutic effects of such power are immeasurable.

Spirit Baptism

According to I Corinthians 15:1-4, the gospel consists of the death, burial and resurrection of Jesus Christ. When we align these elements with the message of Acts 2:38, we discover that repentance answers to death, baptism answers to burial, and the baptism of the Holy Spirit answers to the resurrection. Since the resurrection of Jesus Christ from the dead embodies the ultimate healing over death, then the entrance of the Spirit of God in the believer's life activates the true dynamic of spiritual healing. Power, life, light, revelation, spiritual motivation and many other attributes proceed from the Spirit of God as He indwells the believer. The gift of the Holy Ghost reverses every negative movement and consequence that characterizes sin. For weakness, He gives strength; for darkness, He gives light; for death, He gives life; and for sorrow, He gives joy.

1. **The Holy Spirit generates power for spiritual healing.**

   "But you shall receive power when the Holy Spirit has come upon you; and you shall be witnesses to Me in Jerusalem, and in all Judea and Samaria, and to the end of the earth." Acts 1:8

The world has created and developed many sciences and therapies to help people. Often, health care professionals in physical or psychological fields can pinpoint disorders with great accuracy. They can trace the problems back to their beginnings, identify contributing factors along the way, and project new courses of action to solve them. Unfortunately, it is at this point of implementation and sustained treatment that these programs falter. They cannot make anything happen. They have power to analyze, but no power to energize. They can offer suggestions and support, but the real results are left to the will power of the individual. Also, life cannot exist without energy. Food becomes energy through the process known as metabolism. Our spiritual food (the Word of God) becomes energy through the power of the Holy Spirit. Neither food nor metabolism are worth anything without the other.

> *"Having a form of godliness but denying its power. And from such people turn away!"* 2 TIMOTHY 3:5

Because of this, the gift of the Holy Ghost was conferred upon believers by God to empower them to do spiritual feats. He takes up where religion and reformation fail. He supplies the power to actually implement the changes that must take place in a person's life, plus He gives them power to perform the will of God throughout their lives.

Jesus knew that the baptism of the Holy Spirit was critical to the success of the infant church, both as a corporate body and in the lives of individual disciples. His command to them to return to Jerusalem until they were endued with "power from on high" emphasizes this. He knew that even after training his disciples for over three years, they needed something more. Without the indwelling Spirit they would have a form of religion, but would lack the power to make it work.

2. The Holy Spirit produces life.

Without God's Spirit in a person's heart, spiritual death has the upper hand. The Apostle Paul reasons this out in his epistle to the Romans.

> *"For those who live according to the flesh set their minds on the things of the flesh, but those who live according to the Spirit, the things of the Spirit. For to be carnally minded is death, but to be spiritually minded is life and peace. Because the carnal mind is enmity against God; for it is not subject to the law of God, nor indeed can be."* ROMANS 8:5-7

Physically, when tissue dies, it loses all healing power. As we have seen, dead tissue must be cut away. If it is allowed to remain, it will rot and produce toxic chemicals that will kill the living cells surrounding it. Living cells, however, retain an active blood supply, and can work to bring about healing. Spiritually, unregenerated man is contaminated with sin. Death, then, is present in the soul. Eventually, the entire person will suffer decline and death.

> "For the wages of sin is death, but the gift of God is eternal life in Christ Jesus our Lord." ROMANS 6:23

Life—irrepressible, vibrant, and eternal—holds the greatest healing agent within itself. When a person receives the baptism of the Holy Spirit, he/she is indeed endued with eternal life. Jesus told the woman at the well,

> "But whoever drinks of the water that I shall give him will never thirst. But the water that I shall give him will become in him a fountain of water springing up into everlasting life." JOHN 4:14

Eternal life guarantees eternal victory over death. It is healing raised to the infinite power. And, since the Spirit is God's abiding presence, He works unceasingly in a person's heart and life to bring about positive change. Every day, the Spirit-filled person triumphs in ways both big and small. Death gets over-matched on every front; sin has no place to establish a foothold. As one person has said, "Some people expect to go to heaven at last; I go day by day!" Eternal life does not begin when the last natural breath is drawn. It begins the moment the Spirit of God enters, by faith, into a believer's heart. The Spirit becomes a spring of living water that springs into eternal life.

3. The Holy Spirit connects the believer to the body of Christ.

The scriptures clearly teach that the work of the Holy Spirit is to join a person to the body of Christ. The Holy Spirit gives birth to our relationship with the Heavenly Father.

> "For you did not receive the spirit of bondage again to fear, but you received the Spirit of adoption by whom we cry out, 'Abba, Father.'
>
> The Spirit Himself bears witness with our spirit that we are children of God, and if children, then heirs--heirs of God and

joint heirs with Christ, if indeed we suffer with Him, that we may also be glorified together." ROMANS 8:15-17

Also, the Holy Ghost baptism establishes common ground for the body of Christ, and puts the divine features of Christ into us.

"For by one Spirit we were all baptized into one body—whether Jews or Greeks, whether slaves or free—and have all been made to drink into one Spirit." 1 CORINTHIANS 12:13

Connectivity to the body carries with it all the benefits of the body. Paul elaborates on the functions of the body throughout the twelfth chapter of I Corinthians. Membership in the body facilitates the healing process.

4. The Holy Spirit reveals truth to believers.

Physically, healing depends upon an accurate examination of the disease or injury. If the attending physician overlooks a problem, or diagnoses it improperly, then any prescription for treatment will be off the mark. When the Holy Spirit fills our hearts, He also floods our minds and our consciences with light and truth. Spiritually, He matabolizes truth in our souls. He provides this gift to us because, in our humanity, we are subject to error.

"However, when He, the Spirit of truth, has come, He will guide you into all truth; for He will not speak on His own authority, but whatever He hears He will speak; and He will tell you things to come." JOHN 16:13

Sometimes our mistakes result from ignorance. Sometimes they stem from willful disobedience. In other words, our flesh may rebel against the leadership of the Holy Spirit in our lives. In this regard, the Spirit provokes not only our awareness of the substantive problem, He also provokes our conscience to do the right thing.

"For as many as are led by the Spirit of God, these are sons of God." ROMANS 8:14

5. **The Holy Spirit defends us against the enemy.**

One of the marvels of the Holy Spirit is His role as our Paraclete, or our advocate. In this aspect, He takes over our defense against Satan the same as a defense attorney takes over the defense of a client against a plaintiff or a prosecutor. Indeed, Satan is called the accuser of the brethren, the devil, the tempter, the deceiver, the father of all liars, the Serpent and the Dragon. We need the Holy Ghost to continually fire back answers to the endless attacks the devil launches against us.

> "And I will pray the Father, and He will give you another Helper, that He may abide with you forever—the Spirit of truth, whom the world cannot receive, because it neither sees Him nor knows Him; but you know Him, for He dwells with you and will be in you. I will not leave you orphans; I will come to you." JOHN 14:16-18

Our counselor never rests His case. He never tires of our defense. He never gets stumped or outflanked by the enemy. He provides a flawless defense forever.

> "Therefore He is also able to save to the uttermost those who come to God through Him, since He always lives to make intercession for them. For such a High Priest was fitting for us, who is holy, harmless, undefiled, separate from sinners, and has become higher than the heavens." HEBREWS 7:25-26

In terms of our medical model, the Holy Spirit supplies the antidote to every invasion of our lives by enemy cells. Recalling our discussion of the four lines of defense, God's Spirit immunizes us against the spiritual criminals that seek to re-introduce sin and death back into our hearts.

6. **The Holy Spirit refreshes our spirituality.**

> "But when the kindness and the love of God our Savior toward man appeared, not by works of righteousness which we

have done, but according to His mercy He saved us, through the washing of regeneration and renewing of the Holy Spirit, whom He poured out on us abundantly through Jesus Christ our Savior, that having been justified by His grace we should become heirs according to the hope of eternal life." TITUS 3:4-7

As we consider salvation in terms of its therapeutic value, we see it from a new perspective. We must not see it as a meaningless formality in which we pay nominal respect to tradition. We must not use it to condemn and criticize the unsaved, or to ridicule those who have not precisely fulfilled the requirements, or to stand on as a platform for spiritual pride and superiority. The therapeutic effects make us see salvation from the sinners' standpoint. The sinner pleads for relief from pain, for a lighted pathway to get out of darkness, and for love and hope in an uncaring, desperate world.

Summary and Suggestions

The healing model of salvation encompasses the purpose of Christ. His mission found its fullest expression in saving, healing and delivering sinners from sin. In order to be like Him, our evangelistic thrust must take on the nature and the same driving force that empowered Christ.

> *"For God so loved the world that He gave His only begotten Son, that whoever believes in Him should not perish but have everlasting life. For God did not send His Son into the world to condemn the world, but that the world through Him might be saved. He who believes in Him is not condemned; but he who does not believe is condemned already, because he has not believed in the name of the only begotten Son of God. And this is the condemnation, that the light has come into the world, and men loved darkness rather than light, because their deeds were evil. For everyone practicing evil hates the light and does not come to the light, lest his deeds should be exposed. But he who does the truth comes to the light, that his deeds may be clearly seen, that they have been done in God."* JOHN 3:16-21

This perspective does not absolve us from the obligation to defend the gospel when it becomes necessary. Subversive agents continually work to undermine and corrupt God's Word. This is the reason that many fundamentalists have had to assume a combative posture. Truth has been under modernism's attack for many years. If it were not for ministers who loved the Bible and poured themselves into its defense, the church would have taken huge losses.

Yet, we must avoid the opposite danger of getting locked into a combative mode and forgetting that love motivated Jesus, not hatred. A belligerent mood in presenting the gospel—even in our evangelistic programs—causes us to sow the wrong spirit into our converts. Many new converts would never know about the fights and bitter struggles of the past if those who participated in them would let the matters drop. It's one thing to defend a household with a shotgun; a love affair with the weapon is a different story.

How can *Healing Evangelism* make a difference in you and in your church? While this book is not intended to be a outline for a comprehensive church program, here are some suggestions that will bring a new outlook on the task of reaching the lost.

Please note that these are not suggestions to get out the maps and set up canvassing campaigns or to shuffle paper and fill in the blanks. Plenty of books have been written to help a church in these areas. Rather, these suggestions address the hearts of prospective soul winners. They are called suggestions, not directives, because each soul winner is different and each soul to be won is different. Neither are these the only suggestions that can be made. Look at them, put them in your own words, and come up with ones tailor-made for you. Witnessing must be intensely personal as well as a church-wide activity.

1. **Consider prayerfully and carefully the theme of this book.** This is a book for the attitudes, not for specific actions. It will not work if the basic attitude toward soul winning is not affected. Submerge yourself in the ideas contained here. Get a deep understanding of your mission in terms of healing the souls of men.

2. **Learn the testimonies of the saints around you.** Almost without exception, every person who has been saved in your church came in because he/she desperately needed help. Divorce, addiction, jail, bankruptcy, depression and other problems lay behind each conversion. Learn as many of these testimonies as you can. First, they will confirm what you have read here. Second, they will provide you with true stories to share with hurting people.

3. **Refuse to engage in polemic or combative witnessing.** Every

time you "set somebody straight," you lose a potential convert. An honest discussion of the scripture with a sincere person is fine, but taking on someone who disagrees with you and defeating them in a debate accomplishes little for eternity. It is far better to be seen as the helper, the caregiver, and the one who continually reaches out to the pain in people's lives.

4. **Learn to detect spiritual pain.** Smiles, light conversation, anger, rudeness and many other kinds of behavior helps people hide their pain. Cultivate a keen sensitivity to these signs and minister to hurting people.

5. **Continually portray the gospel as a positive power.** Talk about Jesus as your friend. Talk about your deliverance from pain and heartache. Lift Jesus up as the greatest thing that has ever happened to you. Squelch all negative and complaining talk.

6. **Discover new ways to put substance into your witness.** Meet basic needs of people whenever necessary. Food, clothing and shelter outweigh the words of a witness in the mind of the sinner.

7. **Be a spiritual paramedic.** Prepare yourself to bear the burdens of others. Teach a home Bible study. Pick people up and bring them to church. Sit with people in church. After service, don't run to your friends first and spend precious time talking with them to the exclusion of others. Make your way to the visitors, the sinners and the backsliders.

8. **Incorporate soul winning into your daily and weekly routine.** Schedule in outreach. Plan to do it. Make it as much a part of your life as eating and sleeping. Always be on call. Go out of your way to talk to someone about God.

9. **Re-think and re-word your witness to begin with the sinner, not yourself.** Witnessing is not about you. It is about the sinner and Jesus. Refer to yourself only when it becomes relevant to the

process. Your opinion is worthless to the sinner until you have gained much credibility. Until then, keep the discussion on the person to whom you are witnessing, not yourself.

10. **Structure your church's ministry to meet the needs of hurting people.** Seeker's services are deliberately designed for visitors. They will help to reach out to people without confusing them with issues that have meaning only for church members. Serial Bible studies that deal with problems that the individuals in today's society are facing will give people a good, solid reason for coming to church. A wide range of ministries to reach people who have specific needs or are members of specific groups such as addicts, students or single parents will help to focus in on certain people.

The pulpit must be free to evangelize the lost in every service. This means that the church should never tire of hearing the fundamentals preached or taught. Church members must always be ready to minister to seekers. They also must be ready to teach home Bible studies. They must sacrificially give of their time to reach and win the lost.

Whenever the church sees herself as a caring, helping healing extension of Christ into this world, and whenever the world at large sees the same in us, we will effectively reach the lost.

Illustrations

Page 33	Pain: The Patient's Perspective
Page 40	Shared Symptoms of Sin and Disease
Page 45	Common Painkillers: Advantages and Hazards
Page 47	Shared Reactions of Sin and Disease
Page 51	Recycling Pain
Page 60	Hippocratic Oath
Page 75	ABCs of Urgent Care
Page 80	Holmes-Rahe Stress Test
Page 141	Eight Steps to Spiritual Healing

About the Author

Raised in the Midwest, J. Mark Jordan now lives in Sylvania, Ohio with his wife, Sandy. They have three grown children, all married, and three grandchildren.

Mark earned a Bachelor of Science in Human Relations from the University of Toledo, and has spent his career as a pastor, organizational official and author. He stays busy writing books and articles, speaking at various engagements, and serving as the Ohio District Superintendent of the United Pentecostal Church International. Mark has over ten published books including *Living and Leading* and *The View from the Back of the Pulpit*.

When he has time, he enjoys playing golf. You can read more of his work online at jonathanjordan.squarespace.com.

Other Titles by J. Mark Jordan:

Angels We Have Heard on High: Christmas Reflections
A Short Book about You
Healing Evangelism
LE9oX: Inner Healing – Achievable Spiritual Fitness (with Keith L. Smith)
Learning and Leading in Ministry
Living and Leading in Ministry
Measures of Our Faith: A Survey of Major Biblical Doctrines
Morgan County Morning: A Novel
Morgan County Midnight: A Novel
Sharpening the View
The View from the Back of the Pulpit
They Probably Told Me... But I Wasn't Listening

Our Written Lives
book publishing services
www.owlofhope.com

CPSIA information can be obtained
at www.ICGtesting.com
Printed in the USA
FFOW05n0515091015